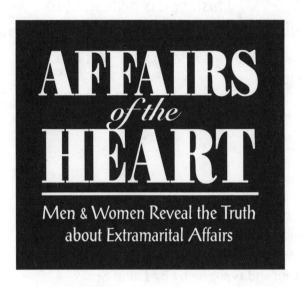

AFFAIRS *of the* HEART

Men & Women Reveal the Truth
about Extramarital Affairs

INTERVIEWS BY

VIRGINIA LEE

THE CROSSING PRESS, FREEDOM, CA 95019

This book is dedicated to
all those who have taught me about love.
You know who you are.

ISBN   0-89594-621-1 (Paper)
ISBN   0-89594-622-X (Cloth)

Contents

Introduction

Opening Pandora's Box

According to Greek legend, Pandora was tempted by her desire to understand the mysteries of life contained inside a holy vial, a "box," which Zeus had forbidden her to open. Driven by her curiosity, Pandora ignored the taboo. Trespassing the boundaries of established order, she defiantly opened the box and released chaos into the world. Her action unleashed a chain reaction, after which life was never the same. Pandora's Box can be a metaphor for what happens to the person who trespasses marital boundaries and becomes irretrievably involved in an affair. Pandora is like the woman having an affair, and her box is like the affair itself.

Having an affair is one of the most transformative experiences a person can go through. One thing is guaranteed—life will never be the same. A fire ignites that changes the person's life forever—for better or for worse—and the process, once begun, cannot be undone. Fortunately, the path is one of self-discovery. For some, the results are devastating. The fallout includes broken marriages and families, shattered careers and dreams, but for others, the results are liberating and serve as a catalyst for tremendous personal growth. People whose lives have been touched by an affair usually fall somewhere between these two extremes.

Many find themselves confused and bewildered, trying to deal with the changes thrust upon them by unpredictable circumstances. Unfortunately, our society provides no models for dealing with this experience. Movies and television don't help. There are no guidelines, no workshops on "How to Have an Affair That Won't Ruin Your Life." The social taboo against having an affair is so strong that ordinary people dare not discuss or even admit what is really happening in their lives. As a result, most affairs are guarded in secrecy with a code of denial so pervasive and powerful that lying becomes a matter of self-preservation.

For a person of integrity, this presents a profound dilemma: telling the truth often means risking everything, yet lying means living in a nightmare of deception. Every person handles it in his or her own unique way. Even experts, marriage counselors and therapists agree that "You have to find what works for you." There are no formulas, no inner road maps showing you the way out. To tell you otherwise would be a lie.

Men and women have been trying to figure out how to love each other since Adam and Eve. Actually, Eve's famed walk through the Garden of Eden with Lucifer was, in a sense, the world's first affair and has been blamed for the suffering of mankind ever since. Love affairs weave a constant theme throughout our history and literature. Consider the love affair between King

Solomon and the Queen of Sheba from the Old Testament, the Greek gods and goddesses of Mt. Olympus, Tristan and Isolde, and Antony and Cleopatra. More modern literature portrays the lost innocence of Hester Prynne in Nathaniel Hawthorne's *The Scarlet Letter*; the self-destructive passion of *Anna Karenina*; and the reckless abandon of *Lady Chatterley*. Dipping into the reservoir of literature allows us to discover those archetypes within—but from a realm of safety. We can identify with and feel compassion for these characters, but when the experience becomes tragic, we can too easily reassure ourselves that it is only a book, and therefore dismiss it as somehow unreal.

For this reason, this collection of interviews portrays the lives of real people with real experiences and real feelings. It is not edited to be comfortable or nice. The underlying motive for addressing this topic is to tell the truth, and in telling the truth, to experience healing from something that touches virtually everyone at some point during his or her adult life. The stories contained within these pages dare to speak the unspeakable. The implicit taboo against those who open Pandora's Box denies support to those who need it most, those who have been wounded, touched, or awakened by having an affair. It's time to bring Aphrodite, the Greek goddess of love, out of the closet. It's time to come out of hiding, open up, and talk about these experiences without moral judgment.

It is not a crime to love someone. Yet falling in love with someone you are not supposed to love may feel like a sin of the highest order. These chapters, through a set of interviews with men and women who have been there, reveal the intricate web of emotions and circumstances involved in the fire of having an affair. In some cases, the fire has purified them, burned away what was dead, and generated new life. Some marital relationships have grown as a result of an affair, bringing in a heightened awareness of love and intimacy. Others bear deep wounds, which may bring deep healing, or which may end either or both relationships. Implied in this book is the affirmation that humans have the innate ability to heal themselves, that the human spirit is capable of finding its own way out of virtually any dilemma.

The positive side of having an affair is the remarkable opportunity to experience the overwhelming power of love, a universal love if you will, a love that transcends moral boundaries. To some, this power is so sacred, so irresistible in its essence, they are willing to risk all that they have.

On the other hand, the chaos of having an affair awakens its own set of demons. Secrecy, of course, is typical because the affair must exist outside conventional societal and moral boundaries. It is this very secrecy that gives magic to the affair but can eventually erode the souls of those involved. Many endure the excruciating nightmare of isolation and self-judgment. Some can lie to protect themselves, and some can't. Some survive, and some don't. Living with untruth has the potential to destroy a person's soul.

Everyone's experience is unique; there is no right or wrong, no absolute analysis as to why an affair happens, no formula for dealing with its outcome, no guarantees. Yet having an affair is a situation that almost everyone faces at least once during adult life.

In the following interviews, you will meet a diverse group of men and women, each of whom has opened Pandora's Box, explored the chaos inside, and embraced the challenge. These men and women had the courage to talk honestly and openly—albeit anonymously—about their experiences.

Who are these people? In these stories, they are your friends, your neighbors, yourselves. The scene is in your own backyard, and you see the participants everyday. They are every man and every woman, ordinary people. The interview process is intimidating and has demanded an interactive openness and vulnerability that is rare to find in most conversation. In reading these interviews, you will have a window into the essence of another person's being—his or her thoughts, feelings, fears, passions, pain and realizations that have awakened as a result of having an affair.

You will not agree with everything you read in these pages, and you will not like everyone you meet. Some you will love, and some you will hate. Some you will cheer for, and some you will cry for. Nevertheless, all of them will awaken your feelings. Please honor what they have been willing to share with you, for it is their truth, and theirs alone. They have dared to expose their most intimate selves.

What the Experts Say

What do the experts say about having affairs? As with anything in life, it depends on whom you listen to. The following comments are from several well-known teachers, counselors, and authors, all of whom are on the cutting edge of what works and doesn't work in relationships. The spectrum of wisdom these experts offer is as broad as the interviews in this book, once again reminding us that no one person, no one expert, no one teacher has all the answers. A good counselor will be the first to tell you that you have to find what works for you.

John Gray is a renowned author and counselor who has been teaching for twelve years about the way to improve relationships. In addition to the 25,000 people he has helped through his seminars, he has written several bestsellers: *What You Feel, You Can Heal*; *Men, Women & Relationships*; and his most recent, *Men Are from Mars, Women Are from Venus*. In a recent conversation, he shared his insights on dealing with affairs.

When a woman doesn't feel that she deserves what she wants, she gives up and is resigned to staying in a lifeless relationship. And when a woman gives up, the man loses too. That's when a man is likely to go out and have an affair. He's usually trying to keep some passion in his life, but he doesn't win that way either. It ends up being a loss/loss situation for both him and his wife. I try to work with couples in a way that allows them to communicate and create a win/win scenario.

When a couple seeks marriage counseling and it doesn't seem to work, that usually means that one of them has a secret he or she won't tell—which most often means that person is having an affair. Having an affair doesn't mean you are a bad person, but it does ruin marriages. When you withhold energy by keeping a secret, the passion goes away. But opening up and asking forgiveness can bring it back.

In the past I would never work with clients unless they were willing to tell the truth about the past to their partners. Now I just ask them to start telling the truth from today. If you had an affair and don't want to tell your partner about it, you don't have to; you can be honest just about the present. As the relationship gets better and better, and trust is re-established, then it becomes safe to reveal the truth about the past.

I don't judge other people for having affairs. It's just where they're at. Personally, I cannot even conceive of having an affair if I am in love with my wife. When I was younger and hadn't learned about the depth of intimacy, I could just go from one woman to the next. Now I can appreciate the beauty of another woman, but it's my wife who turns me on. It's wonderful to become more and more turned on to someone the longer you know her. After years of marriage and living together, I know my wife inside out. Making love with that kind of depth and passion is the most rewarding kind of sex there is.

I believe in marriage as a positive experience, and worth striving for, but it requires a level of maturity that some people aren't ready for. It's not as simple as "Marriage is right, and divorce is wrong, or having an affair is wrong." If you are in a dysfunctional marriage and you are not growing in it, the best thing you can do is to separate. You may need to work on yourself for a while and live alone. Heal yourself first, then you can decide what to do about the relationship. Otherwise you will just re-create the same problems.

Barry and Joyce Vissell have been giving workshops to individuals and couples for almost twenty years and have developed a style of therapy that has evolved out of their own experience. Much of this is documented in their books, *The Shared Heart*, *Models of Love*, and *Risk to Be Healed*. Joyce is very open about discussing an affair that took place twenty-one years ago, an affair that actually helped to launch her and her husband's careers as relationship counselors.

When Barry and I were in our mid-twenties, we had been together for seven years, and married for three. I thought we had a very good relationship. When a friend came to visit who was going through a painful divorce, we graciously took her into our home. Little did I know that she would end up having sex with my husband.

When Barry and my friend told me what had happened, the pain I felt was unlike anything I had ever experienced before or since. All I felt was a terrible sense of betrayal and shattered trust. Instinctively, I realized I could not continue to share my life with Barry if this was the path he was choosing. I locked myself in the bathroom that night, fearing I would kill him if he tried to get close to me. Even the death of a baby years later did not bring as much pain as this.

The next morning I left the two alone together. Honoring a truth I felt deep inside, I packed my bags and walked out of our marriage. Little did I know then that our life path would become dedicated to helping others with healing their relationships.

Barry had no idea what pain or consequences the affair would bring. And now he had to deal with his own sense of loss. Deep pain was welling up in his soul, a pain that allowed him to feel his need for a partner, a pain that would eventually cause major healing and transformation within him. And through my pain, a strength was born within me, a strength to listen to and honor my feelings, a strength I never knew existed.

It took two years to rebuild the trust in our relationship. Though it was the most painful experience of my life, I do not regret it for an instant. We both feel it was the beginning of a deeper, more committed relationship. Before, monogamy was something we took for granted. Now, it is something we practice consciously. The intensity of our love for each other has grown to dimensions never before dreamed of, and the trust we now share keeps the sexual realm of our lives sacred. Ironically, without the fear of either of us having affairs, we are free to love other people.

Many relationships don't survive this fire. In our counseling practice, we try to help others avoid this fire. Yet this very fire can bring about the needed transformation.

In *Risk to Be Healed* (pp. 62-69), Barry expresses his viewpoint on the issue of being intimately involved with other people.

Perhaps the greatest risk we can ever take in our lives is the risk to become intimate with *one* other person. More than sexual intimacy, I mean getting truly close with one other person—not just physical nakedness, but soul nakedness. It's easier to have many acquaintances than to have just one true friend.

People have given us numerous reasons why not to be monogamous. We've been told that it means excluding the rest of the world. We've been told that it's too boring and lacks excitement. We've been told that it's like putting all your money into one investment, and, if it doesn't work, you could lose everything. Perhaps you can relate to one or more of these reasons. I would like to suggest that the fear of vulnerability, the fear of being hurt, and therefore the fear of real intimacy are behind all these reasons.

Does being monogamous mean excluding others? It can. It is possible for two people to isolate themselves from the rest of the world because of fear of other relationships. But for a relationship to remain healthy, it must breathe, giving and receiving love with the rest of the world. A healthy relationship is balanced by openness and accessibility to others.

Then what about sexual openness with others? There is a way to simply let sexual energy, which is the energy of creation, flow through your body and consciousness. This is a wonderful feeling which allows you to be attracted to everyone and everything. Although it is also a physical experience, it is not centered in the genitals, nor is there genital arousal. It doesn't need to be fulfilled by action. It is fulfilling enough to simply let this energy be and experience it.

However, it is easy to fool ourselves into *thinking* we are experiencing this kind of pure, spiritual openness. In an attempt not to exclude others from our primary relationship, sometimes we end up excluding our mate, causing deep pain and contraction in the very relationship we are trying to expand. Sexual affairs are tricky business. Although we can easily rationalize our interest in relating deeply with others, we have the responsibility to be absolutely honest with ourselves and with our primary partner.

What we've discovered in our own relationship, through our own struggles, is that deep trust takes time to develop, especially when it comes to sex. It is something which needs careful cultivating and nurturing. When you allow yourself to act on sexual attractions outside the boundaries of a relationship, you are setting back this process of cultivating trust. It creates a wound that needs to be healed.

Of course there are two sides to every coin. Sexual affairs have brought tremendous growth and change to some couples. Sometimes they have stayed together and healed the wound. Sometimes they have separated. But they have always grown.

In a way, our risking to totally love one another was possible only by risking total loss. Only by risking to lose one another was it possible to more deeply find one another.

Stan Dale is a well-known sexologist who began counseling people on sex, love, and intimacy on a late night radio talk show out of Chicago in the late 1960s. Since then he has given countless workshops to some 30,000 people in countries all over the world over a span of twenty-five years. Stan Dale has also authored two books, *Fantasies Can Set You Free* and *My Child, My Self*. The body of Stan's experience and knowledge is phenomenal and, according to those whose lives he has touched, his counseling works. In a recent radio interview, Stan Dale had some interesting comments on the dynamics of love.

There is either love or a cry for love. Why do we ever take ourselves out of love? Why aren't we in love twenty-four hours a day, seven days a week? What it's really about is energy, and when you are open to that divine energy, you are a radiant channel for love.

And it is the opposite when we are in fear. Fear contracts. Everything in us shuts down and hides. But when we are in love, the energy is flowing, and there isn't anything we can't do.

Once you mention the word *sex*, it's like taking a rattle and throwing it in the middle of an audience. People recoil from the word sex as if it's something dirty, which is too bad since it was designed to be something beautiful, warm, and loving. There really is no such thing as sex. It's a metaphor for how I treat you. If I am a warm, sensitive, and compassionate person, then what I do with any of my body parts is identical. If I am cold and uncaring, then that is exactly how I will make love to you. I will be using you rather than using the energy that we share together. It doesn't really have that much to do with genitals or the few square inches of skin "down there." When I look into your eyes, whether you know it or not, I am having sex with you.

I can love you even if my wife is sitting next to me. My loving you has nothing to do with my wife. Just because I love you doesn't mean I don't love her. Actually, it enhances the love I feel for her. It's simple: When you give love, you get it back. That is the universal nature of love. In truth, which star sparkles more brightly? Which angel is more beautiful?

But most people don't know how to love each other that way, so they get very isolated and lock out the love of others. That's why so many people are starving for love. And that's why people have affairs—to get the love they need. When a marriage breaks up because of an affair, it means that it has stopped growing.

So often in conventional marriages, a couple has gone from being friends to being lovers to becoming man and wife. Once married, the woman becomes her husband's property to love and provide for. Once children are born, the mother often bonds more deeply with her children than with her husband, and he begins to feel that he is nothing more than a cash register to pay the bills. At that point, the husband and wife are no longer "in love" with each other. The roles of "husband" and "wife" have prevented people from being truly in love with each other, and that's when they begin looking for love elsewhere.

The way to avoid that trap is to always remember who you are really in love with. If we are truly spirit in a body, when we are "in love" we are reflections of each other. And if I see you the same way you see me, how can we avoid being in love with each other? I am in love with you.

It's not the kind of love that is demeaning, demanding, or manipulative. So many people think that is what love is. But love is really an open exchange—the ability to be fully open with each other.

Most people are afraid of intimacy because, as a society, we are trained to accept violence more readily than love. Take spanking for example. Consider the parent who says, "I am doing this because I love you," while he or she is beating the child. Spanking should be illegal, yet it is condoned by our society. It's called assault and battery if you do that to an adult. As a society, we are assaulted by violence in the media twenty-four hours a day, And that's why I believe so many people reject warmth and intimacy.

The other form of violence we do to one another in relationships is lying. There are two kinds of lies—the overt lie and the covert lie. The overt lie is just a bald-faced lie. But the covert lie is the lie of omission. It's what I don't say to you. And every time I don't say to you what I need to say, it slowly destroys our relationship. It destroys that bridge we are trying to make between each other's souls. If you want to know why so many relationships fail, just see how many lies are being told every day.

Jealousy is another destructive force in relationships. But all jealousy is the fear of rejection and abandonment; it comes from anger and low self-esteem. Just because you may fall in love with someone new does not mean that you stop loving someone you have loved for a long time. There's always room in life for more love—the true kind of love that doesn't exist at the expense of someone else. It's part of learning how to love as a win/win situation.

Learning how to include the love of other people into what a couple shares with each other doesn't necessarily mean that sex has to be a part of it. Opening up to loving more people can be done in a way that doesn't threaten your existing marriage. You never really have to give up anything, except what doesn't work in your life.

Writer and healer, Joy Gardner-Gordon, also does relationship counseling with her husband, Gordon R. Gordon. Their practice has developed through their own relationship as well as dozens of workshops they have taken on love, sex, intimacy, and communication. Currently they are writing a book on this topic with a working title, "Hanging On Loosely."

They believe that even in the best relationship, no one person can fulfill you on all levels. If you are in a growing relationship, sooner or later you will most likely meet others you will want intimate contact with—intellectually, emotionally, and maybe even sexually. If the original relationship is strong, then you will find that exchanging energy with others can actually enhance the primary relationship. Joy candidly discusses her own relationship.

In the beginning, I felt uncomfortable when Gordon was expansive toward other women. I got anxious and put a lot of pressure on him to pay attention to me. I got what I wanted, but he changed. He was no longer the exuberant, enthusiastic, and flirtatious man I had fallen in love with. I managed to tame him for that first year, but we were both miserable. I discovered that I didn't like him tame. I had fallen in love with a wild man. When he repressed his energy for other women, he also repressed his energy toward me. I wanted back the wild man I had fallen in love with.

I knew that Gordon loved me deeply and had no intention of leaving me. So why did I resent his interest in other women? I did a lot of soul-searching and came up with a theory about jealousy. There are two different kinds of jealousy: rational and irrational jealousy. Rational jealousy is that terrible feeling I get when my husband is talking with a woman I instinctively don't like—someone I can't communicate with, who doesn't care about me, and who might possibly want to take my husband away.

I understood irrational jealousy as the obsessive need to be the only woman my husband finds attractive, and the feeling of being threatened by any attention he shows anyone else. It's the fear of humiliation, the terror of what other people think, the possibility that I am inadequate. I decided that I didn't want my life to be ruled by irrational jealousy any more. I could see that it was literally ruining my marriage.

Gordon responds openly with his viewpoint on their marriage.

As much as I loved being with Joy, I felt trapped. I felt as though I had given up my freedom in order to have a secure relationship. Although it was a good thing, it was stifling. Every time I noticed another woman, she would feel threatened and make me feel wrong for it. I always had to watch what I said and did. I couldn't just relax and be myself. Her attempts to control me made me feel angry and distant. Without even noticing it, I became irritable and critical, which made us fight even more.

Joy finally decided to take positive action. One New Year's Eve, she resolved to try and overcome her irrational jealousy. Although she was scared, she decided to go to a sex, love, and intimacy workshop. After the workshop, she learned that she was able to be with men and women in a very safe but loving way. There was plenty of love to go around. In an environment of abundance, there was no scarcity of or need to compete for love. Being free to express affection with others brought Joy and Gordon closer to each other. She discovered that when she stopped trying to control him, he felt much more loving toward her. When free to express his tenderness toward others, he once again became the man she had fallen in love with. Now she realizes that he doesn't stop loving her, no matter who he is with.

A Lifelong Affair

Some lovers tap into a source of universal love, a passion that transcends conventional rules by fueling the creative spirit. Perhaps that's why many artists over the centuries have exercised the right to have affairs. Yet, how does a respectable person maintain a relationship that exists outside the boundaries of society? In the following interview, Celeste reveals her way of managing to find room in her life for both a marriage and a long-term love affair for more than twenty years.

Celeste

Having an affair may be painful, yet it can also be very sacred, powerful, and passionate. How have you dealt with this paradox?

Having an affair for me involves the whole question of being true to oneself . . . and Self in my mind has a capital "S." It is the same as the soul, the unconscious, that shining core of one's being. The Self has to be the prime focus in one's life. If it isn't, then everything else is lost in terms of integrity. That's where I begin when I think about my relationships. In particular I am talking about a relationship that I have had with a man for twenty-two years.

It began in a restaurant in Berkeley. I had just lost a job, and a friend decided that I could work with Alex very well. So it was arranged for us to meet professionally. When Alex and I met, that was it. You could call it destiny, if you like, to meet such an incredible person on a chance encounter. And that was the beginning of what appeared to be a professional liaison and ended up being a soul connection that has transcended every other level of my life and has lasted for many years. I guess I was in my late twenties when it began.

Were you married at the time?

Actually, I was still married to my first husband, although we were separated. I met Alex at a transitional time of my life; I was between jobs and had just gone through a major death in my family. So I was ripe for change. In the beginning, the relationship was pretty open for me, but it wasn't for him. Alex had just developed a bonded relationship with a woman with whom he has been ever since, although they have never actually married. But they did have a baby, so he had to be fairly circumspect because he wanted to protect his mate.

Can you remember how you felt when you first realized the nature of your connection with him?

Quite easily. As a matter of fact, the energy was very profound at that time and has never changed one iota. It was obviously a deep, sexual energy. It took quite a while for us to actually exercise the sexual option, maybe a couple of months. But it became apparent very quickly that we were to have a very passionate, very sexual love affair. And we did. We maintained this connection on several levels. On one level, we shared professional concerns because of our work and, underneath that, there was a hot love affair. Between those two areas, we were able to come to a deep friendship. And we were able to relate on all these levels successfully.

Early in the relationship, we just had a lot of fun, dropping in on friends. In those days, it was a much freer association. As we both became committed to other relationships, it became more difficult to acknowledge our bond.

How did that make you feel?

I never questioned it, and that has been the hallmark of the relationship. For the most part, I have been able to stay in the moment when I was with him and not give in to my longing for him when I wasn't. Although at several points in my life, when I was unable to nourish myself, I did indeed give in to the longing, wishing, and waiting.

What kept you from wanting it to be more?

Reality. Even at the beginning, I would have never wanted to interfere with what he felt was important to him; I wanted to honor his relationship to his mate and their child. Somehow, I was able do that, even though it was harder for me because I was free. At that point, I also had relationships with other men, so it wasn't as if I was pouring all of myself into this one person.

How did things change when you got married again?

When I married Erik, Alex and I took a break for a couple of years. Although we had a few encounters, my major interest was the relationship with Erik. I was perfectly happy with that. In hindsight, I realize that the relationship I developed with Erik was a very maternally oriented one. I was looking for a man with whom I could have children, and Erik was the one. I went for it and didn't see Alex for a long time.

Did you ever tell your husband about this other relationship?

Absolutely not. There was never any inkling in my mind that I should. I have always reserved a certain part of my life as totally private. That has been another hallmark of my being. I have always maintained a certain amount of independence and sovereignty about my true self. I reserve the right to keep aspects of myself to myself. It is sacred territory.

When did you open Pandora's Box?

Even when I was married and having children, I realized that there was still an unfulfilled energy in me. After an intense period of motherhood when my first child was three, I realized that a very deep energy inside me wasn't being expressed. Although I didn't seek him out, Alex reappeared in my life like magic. There he was one day, sitting on a bench, waiting for a bus. I hadn't seen him for at least three years. Alex met my child, and the energy between us was immediately reawakened. It was a very strong energy, and I believe we exercised it fairly quickly.

At that point things became very difficult. I realized that the part of myself that needed expression was not going to be happy with the conventional taboos that our society puts on having an affair. And it became apparent that it was going to be a challenge not to ignore that part of myself. I was going to have to call on a lot of my resources to sustain an affair in tandem with my child rearing and my relationship with Erik. It was going to be a pretty tricky juggling act.

How did you do it?

I had the wisdom to put the affair on the back burner for years at a time. I could not emotionally handle the guilt and the sheer energy needed to arrange all the logistics necessary to keep it secret. To be in secret communication with Alex became too much of a problem, so I stopped it.

How did the secrecy affect your self-esteem and your ability to be honest with your husband?

For me—and this has been true from the very beginning of this relationship—the element of secrecy has not been an issue. That's because I feel very strongly that a part of me exists separately from any relationship. It's simply a matter of logistics. There's a part of me that believes that what a woman does with her sexual expression really doesn't have anything to do with anyone else. And so I have this way of putting my affair in a separate sphere all by itself.

Are you saying that you feel you have the right to love who you want to love?

Right, and some people in our culture would call that deceit. But I feel that the energy that is evoked in me with Alex has every right to be expressed, and it really doesn't have anything to do with Erik. I simply don't share what is happening to me in one realm of my life, but it's not in a hurtful way. It's kept in its own beautiful little box. And it really doesn't have anything to do with the box next door. One thing has nothing to do with the other. Although it's a difficult thing to continually conceptualize, I have been able to maintain good, strong boundaries in my life around this issue.

How did you learn to develop these boundaries?

It's something I've had to struggle with, but in the struggle I've always managed to keep my mouth shut and not indulge in a conventionally based tendency to tell all. I want something for myself which is separate from every other part of my life. Alex and I have also maintained this separate identity by not discussing our relationships with other people. When we are together, we are together for us. There are no strings attached to anybody else in the world. We are together to discuss and express ourselves as individuals, not our roles as family members.

How would you describe the energy you feel when you are together?

It's very hard to define in words. The best I can do is to explain it in terms of Eros, the "erotic," which is for me the creative energy of the universe. If you can touch that energy through another person, then you are touching the love of the universe. It's a very powerful energy to tap into. Frankly, that's what keeps my affair going. I have never experienced that energy with anybody else in my life, and I probably won't experience it again.

Although this aspect of our relationship is very special, I believe that energy is available for everyone. I think it just depends on how you as an individual want to get that experience. People do it through poetry; some people do it through either playing or listening to music. I do it partially through my art; others do it through their writing. It is available to everyone. And for me, it just happens to be an energy I can find through a relationship to another human being who happens not to be married to me.

Is that why people are willing to risk everything to have an affair?

That's how I feel about it. My relationship with Alex has been through many phases, many levels of difficulty. Several times it looked as though we were through, but there's something that is always there, the depth of that soul connection.

Do you feel that your relationship with your lover transcends the normal laws and boundaries of time and space—and morality?

I think it does. This state of being is so sacred, so instinctual, and so intelligent; it is like everything wrapped into one. There's a level of existence underneath our culture that has set up certain forms, certain boundaries for us to adhere to. Marriage is one of them. But there are certain forces in the universe which are totally unrelated to these earthly limitations. Even though these forms are extremely important for maintaining order and a sense of security in our lives, they are not all we have available to us.

Because of this I have chosen to go beyond or around the form of marriage to experience the essence of this deep, creative energy. And I think the same thing has happened to any woman in our culture who evokes that kind of energy and has it embodied in her soul. We have been taught that it's not okay to express that energy except in the form of marriage. And that attitude has cut us off from an extremely deep reservoir of universal love that can be used to heal the world. And so I feel it's important for people who are having this experience to come out with it, at least in a limited way. They need to be able to acknowledge that they are having this extremely powerful experience. They need to give themselves permission and give the world permission to experience the power of love, which is what we are really talking about.

You don't marry everyone you fall in love with.

Within the context of marriage, does a person still have that right to love someone else?

Yes. And the person has the right to love in many forms. There's the love that mothers have for their children; there's the love of a wife for her husband; then there's the love that lovers share. There are so many forms of love. And somehow we have been told that unless a relationship is sanctified by our culture in the form of a religious ceremony, it isn't valid. That's actually a very dangerous place for us to be in, because it creates great reservoirs of hidden guilt which bind psychic and creative energy. Our world cannot afford that right now.

Why are women who have affairs judged more severely than men?

Basically I think men fear the energy that can be evoked by a woman. In many ways, men are culturally programmed to do this. Men, too, are victims of a patriarchal system that strives to keep women contained. Men don't know what might happen if women unleashed their incredible power to love and create. Our society has always wanted to limit women's expression to very narrow channels. Women have been controlled and owned. It all comes from a very deep fear of the power of love.

In ancient times, there was a matriarchal society where women did not belong to men—and children actually took the mother's name instead of the father's. A woman had the freedom to choose the father of her child, and had the freedom to be the mistress of her own destiny. The shift to the patriarchal society took place with the advent of our current Judeo-Christian tradition. The whole history of that transition is very well-documented in Riane Eislers's *The Chalice and the Blade*.

Is that why affairs have to be kept secret?

This whole issue of having to tell the truth is another way that men and women keep each other under control. Society implies that you're not really a good person unless you tell the whole truth. And it's a truth based on very narrow limitations. Somehow if you don't conform to that truth, then you're a rotten person. You will be excommunicated and ostracized. And that is why you are afraid to reveal that you're having an affair. Automatically, people assume that if you tell that truth, you will be on the outside of everything—your marriage and your culture. The fear is that you will lose everything.

I have to be truthful to myself. Keeping my mouth shut about what's happening is not an untruth. It is simply keeping it under wraps. The flip side of secrecy has this protective aspect to it. Society is not at a point yet where it can accept that realm of a woman's—or a man's—life. There's no support for a person having an affair. Ironically, if people open up and tell the truth, they will be punished. It will destroy their reputation, their marriage, their family. There is tremendous risk in telling the truth. So, for self-preservation, it must be kept secret.

And there is tremendous power in secrecy. It creates the boundaries of an affair. It is paradoxical that we have managed to keep something so important a secret, and at the same time keep it going. One thing that happened to me because of the secrecy was a sense of isolation. As I get more in touch with my sense of self, I am able to reveal more of what is really happening, even if it is only to a small number of women friends—who now know my Truth.

What advice can you offer women—or men—who are suffering from isolation and self-judgment?

My deep respect for my relationship with myself saves me. And that takes precedence over anything else. When I start to feel guilty, which I do occasionally, I essentially ask myself: "Do I want to betray myself, or somebody else?" I cannot betray myself by not expressing this energy that nourishes me so deeply. If I slammed the door on it, my soul would begin to die bit by bit. Or I can just let it express itself in a healthy way in those moments when I can figure out how to let that happen, without hurting anybody. And that's the bottom line for me. I wouldn't think of hurting anybody with the knowledge of what's happening in my private world.

I would tell anyone who is in a moral crisis to tell someone who can be trusted. That will eliminate that pervasive feeling of shame over a kept secret. Those who feel morally bankrupt should probably seriously question their inner strength for carrying this burden.

Some people are not meant to have affairs. Anyone who does not have a good relationship with him or herself will suffer greatly. Anyone who cannot stand the heat of an affair shouldn't have one. Having an affair means playing with fire. Without adequate understanding of this energy, you will get burned clear through.

What do you think would happen if your husband found out?

A couple of things could happen. In my relationship, there's a strong possibility that our marriage could contain that information should it be revealed. In some ways it would be a growth opportunity. I would love to be able to share that deep part of me that needs expression, even at such a high risk. Erik might just be able to understand it. It could allow us to try and express that energy in our relationship. But because the affair is so powerful in its current form, I don't even want to change the nature of my relationship to Erik.

How would you feel if you found out that your husband had been having an affair?
Aside from our having a common bond, I can honestly say that I don't know how I would feel. I think we would be on the same wavelength about a lot of things and wouldn't have to go into many explanations.

Do you feel that your ability to love your husband has deepened as a result of your affair?
Infinitely. The affair is so deep and so transcendent that it actually fuels all my relationships: with Erik, with my children—and even more important—with my art. The passion fuels my creativity. I use this energy as a muse. When I can tap into the way I feel when I am with that person on a sexual level, it is extremely powerful. I wish it could be bottled and sold. But how could you ever put a price on it?

Interestingly enough, my affair has paralleled my inner life as a person. It has followed me on my path of personal growth. In the past, I've externalized it, saying it's the relationship that's evoking this energy in me. But now I can see it comes from me; I am evoking this creative energy out of myself, and the relationship is but a reflection of this energy. And that means that I don't know about the future of my affair in the end. I may totally claim my ability to evoke that energy myself. But, somehow I doubt I could give it up altogether, because it has been extremely enjoyable.

If you found out you had six months to live, would it change things?
I would make sure I had more opportunities to express that energy, but I wouldn't change the outward appearance of my life.

What has been the gift of your affair?
Somehow we are able to give each other exactly what we need, whether it's a sexual connection, emotional comfort, a discussion about professional life, or where I am at with my art.

It has been an incredible two-way street. The relationship has been a supportive exchange between two intelligent and gifted friends who are able to tell each other about what they are seeing and feeling. It has been a gift to have such an intense relationship so full of clarity and integrity. We are able to be our finest selves with each other. Over the years, the sexual aspect of the relationship has become secondary to the love we share.

Celeste 17

Can you find that same quality in your marriage?

I think what happens in a marriage—at least what happened in my marriage—is that the pure connection is there initially. But when habits, and time, and children, and responsibilities wash over a marriage, some of the clarity, intensity, and integrity diminishes. But I assume that if those qualities were at the core of the marriage to begin with, they could be retrieved. If the basic chemistry was there once, it can be there again.

What is your opinion of monogamy?

In reality, in everyday life, we have only a certain amount of energy. I know that I have only enough energy for these two people.

What if your lover came to you having decided that he wanted your relationship to be a primary one?

Although on occasion I have fantasized how wonderful that would be, I go right back to reality and realize that there's no way I would give up the integrity of my family life for my love—no matter how strong it is. Something tells me that the life of my children and their sense of wholeness in being part of a family are also sacred. Recently—and I had to do a lot of soul-searching—I decided that I would give up the relationship before I would give up my family. If I had to, I could evoke that energy in other ways. But I will never give up the energy itself.

What are your thoughts about serial monogamy?

For our love relationships to be expressed in a truly integrated way, we would probably not be married to the same person for our entire lives. I think we would marry once as a practice run, marry again to have children, and then perhaps choose another mate for our later years. Many people actually do this. Some people get married five times. There are so many levels and phases of life that need to be explored. It's difficult to expect one person to be there for all of them.

Do you think that people outgrow each other?

Yes, I do. It is easy to maintain the illusion of a lengthy marriage. But it is rare to find the couple that is truly able to continually relate in a whole and integrated way. As a human species, I don't know if we are well developed enough to make those transitions in a truthful way. And culturally, we are not raised to be aware of our inner life. As women, the conventions of society always define our roles.

What has happened to the women who have ventured outside the respectable boundaries of their marriage?

It seems that these women have often dared to taste the forbidden and then, if found out by society, suffer tremendous guilt. They feel that they have done something terribly wrong, and they retreat back into their lives thinking that somehow they ought to be punished.

I grieve for these women very deeply. I grieve for the judgment they feel has been passed on them without any kind of trial, and for their guilt as some form of penance. I grieve that they feel unworthy as a result. These women are guilty only of exploring their own sexuality. What's wrong with that? I really admire a woman who can experience herself in an empowering way, in a liberating way—yet preserve the integrity of her marriage. At the same time, she can grow inwardly as a human soul, without sacrificing who she is to suit society's conventions and demands.

This is the essence of the paradox I have been trying to understand in my life—the nature of the taboo, the nature of the forbidden. It's ironic that the very thing that can nourish us is the very thing we are not supposed to have. And there's a certain frustration with a situation where in order to be whole we have to trespass beyond certain boundaries. It takes a tremendous amount of courage to take that risk, to go against what society tells you is okay, and to still feel whole within yourself. I believe that we have the divine right to experience love beyond society's boundaries.

It's amazing that for centuries—actually millennia—artists, poets, and other great and colorful people throughout history have had affairs. Look at the love story of King Solomon and the Queen of Sheba. It's right in the Old Testament. Nevertheless, there is still a level of social condemnation toward these people.

Pandora had to defy what was forbidden to open the box and, today, we have to defy the social order to tap into this creative yet chaotic power.

Do you think it's necessary that our social order puts a frame around these bounds of passion?

Yes, or life would be absolute chaos. It's a lot like framing a piece of art. Maybe the secrecy of an affair is the boundary around the love that makes it so powerful. The affair, the passionate relationship may be in itself a work of art that needs secrecy as its frame.

If you had it to do over again, would you?

Without a doubt. I can't say that I would have done anything any differently. Actually, I sometimes wonder, had I met Alex six months earlier and had the opportunity to marry him, if I would have done so. And truthfully, I doubt it, based on our personalities. As a match, we are too similar. We would have never gotten anything done in our lives.

How did you experience the chaos of opening Pandora's Box?

The hardest thing to let go of was my desire for a permanent union with that fiery passion. It's easy to want that intensity in life all the time. But that's not how life is. At times it has been very painful for me to have to go back to the reality of my life, to go home.

It's important to find what you need in the moment and allow it to heal other parts of your life. So, in essence, I always have that passion, that fire within me. The ultimate challenge is in learning to contain it. And the pain is always there too. It comes up regularly. I continually go back to the reality that it might not be wise or possible to have that amount of fire and passion in my life all the time. It might totally consume me. Or if I had it every day, the flame might go out and then it would be over. I have to remind myself of that all the time.

Has jealousy touched your life as a result of all this?

You have to know how to withstand the force of jealousy if you are going to operate in this arena. There's a very negative side to jealousy but, on the positive side, it is really just an affirmation of passion. Although it can be ugly, jealousy is just the flip side of love and desire. From my point of view, indifference is worse than jealousy.

How do you deal with people who think having affairs is immoral?

I just turn a deaf ear to them. I believe there is a morality much higher than their arguments—one based on universal love. I have to serve my own truth.

What do you think of other people who have affairs?

The most important thing about having an affair is to know what your motivations are. You need to have a very clear mind about why you are doing it. If you have an affair out of a neurotic need to fulfill yourself in someone else, that is a very ill-conceived reason and probably won't get you very far. The same is true if you're using an affair to get even with someone else who has hurt you, or if you're just bored. There are many motivations for having an affair that I wouldn't honor. For me, the bottom line is whether or not you are having an affair from a sacred place in your heart.

Is it easy or hard to talk about having an affair?

There's a vulnerable part of me that comes up when I talk about this love affair because it's a very deep relationship. I don't talk about it with very many people, and only a few people in my life know about it.

What are your feelings for Alex?

Respect, pure and simple respect. He embodies an integrity that's unusual. Alex has a deep connection with the good within himself. Then there's the delight, the humor, and the fun. Yet we always face the truth in each other with naked honesty. There's a lot of joy when we're together.

What have you lost as a result of the affair?
The major loss for me has been my serenity. When I have been with Alex, the pot's been stirred, the soup is on . . . it's boiling. But perhaps that's just the hallmark of a creative person. Maybe that's why artists and poets always seem to have affairs.

Do you think having affairs is a normal part of life?
No, I don't. It's a normal way of life for some people, but there's a vast majority who probably shouldn't have affairs. Some people have affairs, bringing nothing but destruction and chaos. It all comes down to your purpose, inner strength, and awareness. Having an affair demands a certain level of consciousness to contain the information so that no one gets hurt.

Is there anywhere to find support for this process or does it come completely from within?
Fortunately, today, we all have certain people in our lives with whom we can share the truth. It really takes only a few. In the past, though, many people used a diary or journal as their confidante because they could not reveal the truth of an affair. Adultery was a very heavy crime for which women were burned, stoned to death, disinherited, and ostracized from society. Today if you need the support, you will find it.

Do you think that this affair will ever end?
After twenty years of being involved with Alex, through all the pain and pleasure, all the highs and lows, this relationship is obviously meant to be. I became aware of that fact only about a year ago.

On several occasions when it became too hard for me to keep this going, when the pain of separation was too intense, I've given it up. And every time I've tried, I realized that it is something that just won't die. No matter how many times I've tried, it just hasn't worked. A year ago, I conceded that I wasn't ever going to pull out. I guess you could call that a lifetime commitment.

How do you sustain the passion of your affair?
I just keep going back to it. It sustains itself, and it never goes away. That kind of ever-present divine energy is really what surrounds us all the time. It's not all that unusual; it's a perfectly normal state of being. Many of the ancient matriarchal cultures recognized this. The Druids had the fires of Beltane, the Greeks had the Dionysian feasts, the Romans had vestal virgins and temple priestesses, as a way to ritually tap into that divine, creative source of Love.

Philosophers and psychologists call it "Eros." Carnaval and Mardi Gras are all we have left today of those ritualistic love festivals. It's amazing to remember a time when the world celebrated love instead of war. Maybe that's why for thousands of years we women have had to go underground with the passion, the love that is our divine nature.

Forbidden Fruit

Married for many years to a devoted wife whom he loves, Steve even so found it natural to want affairs. He exercised tremendous discretion to keep his affairs secret to protect his wife, his lovers, and himself. Offering a candid male perspective, Steve explains how having an affair can work to the mutual benefit—he believes—of everyone concerned.

Steve

Having an affair is a theme that runs throughout classical literature—from King Solomon and the Queen of Sheba to Tristan and Isolde. Yet even in our supposedly liberated age, it is a difficult thing to talk about. Why do you think this is true?

The openness and awareness of the sixties and seventies seems to have died in the backlash of the Reagan era in the eighties. I've seen this reflected in many different facets of life, from architecture to social mores. It's a pendulum that seems to swing back and forth. But each time the pendulum swings back, it doesn't swing back quite as far back as before.

Why do you think there is such a paradox between marriage and having affairs?

Thou shalt not commit adultery is one of the Ten Commandments. You find people who are equally jealous and possessive no matter what their viewpoint. The desire to own and to bind is very strong. I believe that the whole binding system was something invented by females to raise children. Women want to keep their mates around to help raise the young. So they get married, and it's against the rules to leave or to love anyone else.

I believe that males don't really care about monogamy. In marriage, I think that men feel just as owned and controlled by women, as women do by men. Marriage in general is something perpetrated by women, while a man's true nature is to impregnate as many women as possible.

Strong taboos have brought us to where we are today, but they haven't stopped people over the centuries from doing what it is natural for them to do.

So you think these taboos exist just to keep the family intact?

I think that's a very strong reason. For example, the Jews don't eat pork, not because it's a blasphemous food, but because pork came from diseased pigs. To protect themselves, they made dietary rules, which then became religious rules. Similarly, the taboo on having affairs involve social and religious rules to protect the family. We actually seem to be losing sight of the family in today's society. A lot of families are breaking up. There are women who work and want careers. They want to be equals with men.

Yet there are societies very different from ours. In certain cultures, polygamy is necessary for the survival of its society. There is a different set of rules about sexual ownership. Even in the Afro-American culture, a father's responsibility for his child is not so ingrained. It's much more of a matriarchal society.

For a man, is having an affair simply an issue of sexual conquest?

There are lots of motives for having affairs. For some, it's just a fresh connection. Others find themselves with the wrong mates and fall in love with someone else. For various reasons throughout history, many married people have stayed together by having affairs. I think this was especially common in Victorian and Edwardian England.

You read novels about people who conveyed just in a glance the strongest of emotions possible. These may have been affairs that were never consummated. Yet for twenty years, a couple may have had a passionate feeling for one another.

In your mind, why do people do this?

Usually there's an electromagnetic chemistry between a couple that leads to an affair—pure instinct and curiosity. Now that more people are working and living independently, there is more opportunity to get together with someone. Society really is a lot looser than it used to be with no-fault divorces. People don't seem to consider marriage to be that permanent anymore.

Marriage does offer security and a deeper knowledge of one person, but for that you give up the freshness. People like to have both.

Does passion make people crazy? Why do people risk having affairs knowing how much pain and suffering it brings into their lives? Do you think people break the rules just for the thrill of it? It's not a logical thing to do.

Human nature is irrational. Usually people don't fully anticipate the consequences of what they do. We all drive too fast on the highway, and the consequences for that could be death. That ought to make everyone slow down, but it doesn't. It's human nature to pursue feelings and to have deep emotions.

Does it take a certain kind of person to risk all he or she has to experience an affair?

I don't think so. I think it's a latent quality in almost every type of personality; it runs the gamut from bookworms to daredevils.

Do you think that this is an inevitable part of human nature? Does this happen to most adults at some point in their lives?
Yes. At least the spark happens, the desire happens even if people don't follow up on it. Different societies have different degrees of control over that desire, even if it just gets acted out through eye contact. Maybe the desire gets acted out in one wild night of passion, and maybe it gets acted out over a number of years. Even Jimmy Carter admitted that he had "lust in his heart." From my experience, everybody feels it and everyone responds differently.

Where do you think all the guilt and punishment comes from?
It's all a morality play. Even in the time of Hester Prynne and *The Scarlet Letter*, people were getting together like stray dogs. And now we have AIDS. It's seems to be the ultimate punishment for the era of free love we experienced in the sixties and seventies.

It's all a matter of what I call raging hormones. They peak in different people at different times of their lives. The chemical basis for our emotions, I believe, is something that is little understood: what turns you on, what turns you off, how it gets turned on, and how it feels to different people. The study of human emotional chemistry is so variable it would be hard to reduce it to any general stereotypes.

Do you think people should be quiet about their affairs or go home and tell all?
I think people ought to keep quiet, absolutely—it's the wisdom of the ages. Although there are cases when it works to tell all. The crisis, the catharsis, and the purge can serve to pull a marriage together; as often as it breaks it apart, it pulls it together.

But overall, it's best to stay quiet. Your partner must not know, whereas many of your friends may know. And that is probably the biggest betrayal— more than the actual affair itself.

Do you think that it's feasible for everyone to know?
Not in today's society, not under the rules we play by. It's just not allowed. If it comes out, you may be in a position where you have to make a choice. And breaking up the family is not a good thing to do in these times. So, it depends on the people involved and their responsibilities. It gets down to the issue of fatherless children, who may end up as the refugees of an affair. You have to consider the end result. The children have not acted irresponsibly, so why should they have to pay for it?

As a man, is your loyalty as a provider for your family more important than what is happening in your personal life?

Yes. There are things bigger than personal feelings. Selfishness is something we all balance—our needs against larger needs.

Do you have a judgment against people who choose an affair over a marriage?

Historically, people have stayed married with divorce never even an option. Affairs were an outlet for people in a marriage to someone they weren't in love with. People didn't get divorced. And a lot of those affairs were reasonably open and went on for a long time. There are places—like Latin America—where that is an accepted way of life. It keeps the family together, and makes allowances for human nature.

What do you think of societies where there is a double standard? Some societies accept that it's okay for a man to have an affair, but if a woman gets caught, she suffers severe consequences.

Women have to fight for their rights. Some women's groups over the centuries in various cultures have done better than in others. Iraq was secularized fifteen years ago until they were recently bombed back into the Stone Age. And in Algeria today, there is a civil war between secularism and fundamental Islam. It's the classic struggle between church and state, and when the state wins, it is almost always better for women.

The reality is that women have to take what they can get, because no one's going to give it to them. It's never given to anybody. The world is in constant competition, species-wise, gender-wise, business-wise. Sociologically, that's what's happening to countries and tribes and cultures worldwide. Just as bigger companies absorb the smaller ones, the smaller tribes either have to assimilate or get wiped out. Just as people are willing to die for their freedom in Iraq and Algeria, women have to fight for what they want. The Suffragettes were a fine example, but the struggle isn't over. Women have to take their own power.

Prior to 1955, no woman could join the National Press Club. Prior to 1971, women weren't allowed to be members but were allowed to stand in the upper gallery. Meanwhile, the men were downstairs eating a four-course meal, and asking questions across the table. Then came such women as Barbara Walters , Jane Pauley, Connie Chung. These privileges don't come through any blossoming of consciousness; they come through protest, argument, and taking power. I don't think you can get away from the competitive instinct of human nature.

How tolerant society is of having affairs is a matter of degree, ranging from stolen sidelong glances to a harem of concubines. But the instinct never goes away.

What do you think of love triangles, like the kind Henry Miller was involved with in Paris during the twenties? Do artists and writers have poetic license to express their sexuality however they please? It seems that society gave them permission to do that.

No, society didn't give them permission; they were outcasts. They were bohemians by choice. It's only in looking back that they have become lionized. They didn't want approval; if anything, they wanted disapproval. But again, it was during an era of new art, new expression, and new ways of living. So, they experimented with triads. But three is an unstable number. I think it's only because their writings have become famous that people tolerate their antics. Once again, it's an example of stretching society's rules until there's a backlash.

On a personal level, would you describe yourself as monogamous?
No.

Do you think that having an affair is immoral?
No.

What do you think of people who have affairs?
Good and bad. I see people do stupid things. I learn quite a bit from people I've seen having affairs. I'm just interested in the human condition. I don't put value judgments on people's actions.

Have you ever had an affair?
Yes. It's something that I try not to talk about.

Why?
I really don't want my personal business out in the open. I'm not the kind to have a one-night stand. I don't pick up people in bars. The last time I had an affair, the woman knew me and knew I was married. Over a period of time, we got closer until we had an affair.

How long did it last?
Almost a year.

Do you believe it's possible to have an affair that would last throughout your life?
For me personally, no, but I do think that happens for a lot of people. My affair happened out of a selfish desire to gain some experience—I guess at the expense of my integrity.

For me, it's a short-term experiment in the first place. Generally, when both people know that it's not a permanent thing there's not a lot of deception.

I have never promised to get divorced in order to marry someone else. Generally, people take what they want as long as it's useful to them.

Have you ever considered leaving your spouse for someone you were involved with?
I've considered leaving her for other reasons, but not because of another woman.

Has anyone ever asked you to do that? Has that ultimatum ever ended an affair for you?
No.

Did this last affair have a negative affect on your life ?
It has created problems in my marriage, and there was an ending with someone I cared about. There's a sense of loss.

Has your wife ever confronted you about having an affair?
Yes. We were able to talk it out. She waited until after it was over to confront me about it, when it was pretty well diffused. She had accepted it and knew it was over, and she let me know that she knew.

How do you think she would feel if it happened again? Has she accepted that this is just who you are?
Neither of us believe that there will be another affair. But that's probably just wishful thinking, since I am such a devoted student of human nature.

Do you still miss the woman whom you last had an affair with?
Pretty much. Sometimes it hangs on for a long time, and sometimes it's bittersweet after that. It's no different than any other relationship, whether you're married or not.

What did you gain from the experience?
Experience. Knowledge of how people act, and why people do things. It's the human condition that I am interested in.

Did you feel as though you were a different person after the affair?
Yes, but I don't think that there has been a profound change in the direction of my life.

What did you lose from the experience?
Not very much. There's always pain, but then life is full of pain. I really have everything I want. I've never really had to sacrifice anything.

Is it something you would do again?

I'm not planning on it at this time, but human nature being what it is, I can't make an absolute prediction. Who knows what's out there, but right now, I don't feel the need to have affairs. Maybe my hormones have just calmed down. On some basic level, I'm satisfied.

What do you think about open marriages?

My observations are that most of them don't work out. Most of the open marriages I have seen end up in failure. It seems that the most productive way to get on with life is to stay married and have discreet affairs on the side, within the boundaries of what your society will tolerate. To me, that is the wisdom of the ages.

The bohemians of the twenties, the hippie communes of the sixties, all these living experiments just don't seem to work as efficiently. There are other things to do in life other than just having affairs and relationships. There's value in having a social system that runs fairly smoothly, and accommodates as many aspects of human nature as possible.

Do you think it's possible for us to evolve as a species where partners could comfortably come and go in a relationship?

No, I don't think we will ever evolve to that point. I don't think people can control their lives and set their limits. It's easy to say that, but what happens when Mom brings a boyfriend home while Dad's away on a trip? Kids need ordered lives. They like to live like Wally and Beaver or Ozzie and Harriet; they want an ideal TV sitcom family life. And that's how children feel secure, having a mother and father around in a stable situation. Even though security is an illusion, I think you've got to make some semblance of it while you're raising kids.

Do you think it's possible for a marriage to tolerate relationships with members of the opposite sex, even if sex is not the primary part of it?

In most relationships, sex is way down on the list. What you are talking about is human companionship. I would say that people who have affairs actually spend very little time having sex. It's a lot more on an emotional level; it's having someone you feel you can talk to.

The idea that you can be true to one person, and tell all about your other relationships is social chaos. You may as well all meet each other and go out to dinner. To me, it's more emotionally and socially efficient to meet discreetly and observe the boundaries of an ordered marriage. I don't do it out of any religious or moral commitment. It just happens to be what works.

What seems to work the best is to stay committed, stay married, and to have a high tolerance for what happens on the side. I'd like to see less divorce, and more staying together. Controlled affairs keep society intact. But then there are so many people who can't control themselves, who are flagrant and have no discretion in their lives.

How has the element of jealousy affected your life?
My wife had an affair with a good friend of mine before we were married, and I wasn't jealous. I'm not the jealous type. She's not particularly jealous either. It has more to do with security issues.

How would you consider the trust between you?
We've always had pretty good trust between us.

Does having an affair affect that trust?
That's one little box. I can be trusted to continue providing money for the family, to be a certain kind of father, to keep doing the things that make our lives run.

If she asked you about your affairs, what would you say?
I would be truthful and have been truthful about what has happened in the past. I would probably deny an affair happening in the present.

Where does that denial come from?
A desire not to deal with it.

What are you afraid of?
I'm not afraid of anything. I just don't think that bringing it out in the open works. Sometimes having it all out brings you closer, and you promise that it will never happen again. But what happens ten years down the road when you find yourself in the same situation all over again?

I don't think that's a way to get past the problem. Let's not talk husband and wife, but just relationships between men and women. In most relationships, neither one really wants to have an affair, but one stumbles and does something he really didn't want to do within his philosophical framework. Even devout churchgoers who believe that adultery is a sin are still adulterous. There is no evidence that Christians are any *less* adulterous than anybody else. Then they go to church on Sunday and confess; they are devoutly sorry for indulging in this forbidden pleasure they are experiencing. Maybe that's why it's so wonderful.

In my observation, once an affair comes out into the open—unless there is a complete reversal and promise of eternal faith and trust—the marriage usually ends in divorce.

So, my advice is to just keep a lid on it. There are four billion people on this planet. Each of us might only meet a few thousand, and only know a few hundred, and maybe only love a few of those. So, the idea of one true love is totally absurd to me.

So, one relationship can be as good as another. If you moved to the Sudan, you could probably still find someone to love. There's got to be a pretty serious reason to trade one relationship in for another. I don't see that you're going to find true love in some affair that comes along, because your marriage was a mistake, although I have seen it happen.

How would you feel if you found out your wife was having an affair?
It would depend on how it affected me. If it was in the past, it wouldn't affect me at all. If it were happening today, I would mostly be concerned about how many people know about it. I would hope she would be discreet.

Would you let her play it out?
Would I have much choice?

Would it relieve any guilt in you?
No, not at all.

Would you ask her to give it up?
Probably. It comes down to my security. Will I have someone to take care of me into my old age, or will she be leaving me for him? I would want to know now. You can't expect someone you had an affair with twenty years ago to take care of you when you are sick or dying. I would never let one of my affairs threaten the security of our marriage.

If you want that kind of security, you need to hang in there. It's a mutual pact you enter into—for better or for worse, for richer or for poorer—and I don't think the occasional affair takes away from that long-term commitment. Unfortunately, I think people throw it away all too often for very mundane reasons. There are too many lonely old people sitting in their apartments who have no one to talk to.

What about sex? Is it better in an affair than it is at home? Is it sexual curiosity that fuels the affair?
Women seem to have better sex when there are feelings of long-term trust and intimacy. As a man, I've had great sex both ways. Maybe the best was a one-night stand in my twenties, but in the long run that's not what's important to me.

How do you feel about this topic coming out in the mainstream?
I feel that it's definitely worth talking about. But I am not calling for a radical change in society to acknowledge all this stuff. Society has rules that make things work smoothly. They are limiting in a lot of ways. But from my experience, total freedom is total chaos.

Between Two Lovers

There are times in a person's life when an old lover reappears, when the past can be more irresistible than the present—especially if the present is in a state of chaos.

This is the story of Suzanne who ran into an old lover one night while her husband Richard was out drinking with his buddies. Seeing Tom again revived old feelings, and made her even more aware of her growing discontent with her marriage.

Suzanne

Why did you have an affair?

I think it had a lot to do with being unhappily married for quite some time. I made the mistake of trying my hardest to make sure that everyone else was happy—except myself. I always put my husband's needs before my own. He would go out drinking with his friends and not come home. He just wouldn't show up when he said he would, and gradually the resentment built up. For a long time he could not understand how I felt: my sadness, my loneliness, my feeling upset. It just made him angry, and he would say resentfully, "What's your problem?"—as if I was not allowed to have a problem. We both have problems. We're both human.

We had not been connecting for several years. We were both working hard to meet the mortgage on our house, but we weren't really paying attention to what was making us happy or unhappy. It all started one Friday night, when he didn't come home. I rented a video and picked up some pizza for dinner. I waited and waited, but he didn't come home, so I called him. He said, "I'll be home right away. I'm just leaving."

I said, "Don't bother. There's no hurry, because I'm going out." I went out by myself and happened to meet an old friend I hadn't seen for eight years. Before I was married I had a romantic relationship with Tom and hadn't seen him since. It was nice to get some attention from Tom who seemed genuinely happy to see me. I was so angry and fed up with Richard that I didn't care anymore. Tom and I just danced and talked until the place closed, and then I went home. Even going out alone to a club was something I had never done before. That act was a statement in itself. I gave Tom my business card and we agreed to meet for lunch. It wasn't long before we began to fall in love again.

Did Tom become your confidant for the problems you were having in your marriage?

Yes, he did. He knew my husband and understood what he was like. The three of us had once been friends. We once lived in the same house, with Tom and his ex-wife, but Tom and Richard were no longer friends, so Tom was very much on my side. He felt that Richard was selfish and that he hadn't been treating me right.

How did the affair affect your marriage?

After two months, I told Richard I was having an affair, and he figured out that it was Tom. I was so in love, I didn't really care how it would affect him. Since I had spent my whole marriage worrying about how he felt, it was very liberating. I had the day off and spent all afternoon at the beach with Tom. Richard sensed that something was up. I knew that Richard knew, and so I decided not to go on pretending anymore. I had a glass of wine and was taking a bath. Richard came in to talk to me and asked what was going on. I told him that I had been seeing someone for about a month. He asked me for details like how often. I was surprised that he wasn't mad, just pensive. Then he said, "I can't be angry, because I have had two affairs myself." He confessed everything to me, something he never would have done before. My confession opened up a door for him.

How did that make you feel?

It made me feel justified. No wonder I had felt abandoned and unhappy for the past two years. He said he had never told me because he was afraid I would leave him.

What was the result of being honest with each other?

Since we both had known each other for so long, we were able to tell each other all the details. At first, the honesty felt so strange and good, it was almost exhilarating. That we could be that way together made me think that maybe there was a chance, but now I feel that the truth may have been too much for either of us to ever completely trust each other again.

Did he insist that you end the affair?

No, it was not that direct. He just told me that he loved me and that I was his soul mate. He was *very* distraught. He was ready to go into a Zen monastery, become celibate, and never be with anyone again. Or maybe run away to Europe, or drive off a cliff on his motorcycle.

Do you think he was punishing you for his affairs?

I think so. He had a lot of guilt. He felt responsible that it happened, because he was the first to have an affair.

Were his affairs finished by this time?
Yes, they were; they had been for a year.

Why did he continue to go out and leave you at home?
He says it was because of his guilt.

What did you do next? Go to counseling? Go out on more dates?
He started wining and dining me. He became the most loving and gracious man you could ever expect a husband to be. And it just confused me. It's not what I wanted from him right then. It felt like bribery, and it made me feel guilty.

Did you continue seeing your lover?
My feelings for Tom were so strong that I tried to be with both men for a few months; then it got to be very difficult. I could not stand the deceit and deception. I began to think that there was something wrong with me, that I was a bad person.

When did it get to the crisis point?
Richard had given me an ultimatum not to see Tom anymore, but I never complied with it. All I said is that I was willing to try. I still wanted to be with Tom even though Richard was wining and dining me. I wanted him to leave me alone so that I could figure out what I wanted to do. I tried to move out, but it was so emotionally painful—I couldn't abandon Richard.

How did you leave your lover? Did you tell him you didn't want to see him anymore?
I never told him that, but he became very distant. All communication had to come from me. I have always been the one to initiate the contact with him. It's strange to be the one in pursuit.

Has he ever pressured you to leave Richard?
No, he never has. He has always said that I should, but he hasn't asked me to leave Richard for him. I believe that he wants me to come to him freely, not on the rebound. He knows Richard, and he wants us to work it out if we can—or for me to leave him if we can't. And I can't seem to do either.

That's quite a dilemma. Do you still talk to him?
Sometimes once a week, and sometimes not at all.

Is there someone else in his life?
I don't think so. I think he dates, but he's never told me he was in a new relationship and not to call him.

Do you have a feeling that you and Tom are destined to be together?
This happened before, thirteen years ago, under very similar circumstances. Richard and I were together for a very short period of time. He went off to study at a university without me, but he still wanted me to be his girlfriend. Even then, Tom was upset and didn't think Richard was treating me right.

Tom dropped by for a visit one Friday night and asked why I was alone. When I told him I was waiting for Richard, he said, "Well, you shouldn't be waiting for him because he's out at a party with somebody else." At the time, I was so in love with Richard, it totally crushed me and made me really angry. As a result, Tom and I had an affair that lasted a few weeks. Richard moved away. Then I got a call from Richard, who decided that he wanted me to move in with him again. So I just up and left. At the time, that is what I wanted to do. From then on, I always felt like I was the giver and he was the taker. I was so in love with Richard, I wanted to be with him even though it hurt a lot. But for years, Tom was my fantasy. I used to think about him all the time.

Have you ever thought that this man might offer what Richard does not—that you deserve to have this kind of love and understanding?
I was happiest when I had both. I felt fulfilled, independent, happy, and very selfish. But in reality, that is not possible. It would be difficult to create an honest relationship with my lover based on these circumstances. I don't want to have to hide.

Did you ever separate from your husband?
Emotionally, yes. I've really changed as a result of all this. I've become hard in my honesty, and I know it's really hurt Richard's feelings. He was expecting me to fall in love with him again and I just couldn't. I asked Richard to leave repeatedly and he never did. About three months later he decided that he had to. An opportunity came up that was convenient for him. What happened then to my astonishment is that our relationship got better, and we became better friends. It was wonderful to have my own place and still have him in my life.

Were you still seeing your lover, too?
Yes. That's when things were the best. I felt better about myself and didn't want my husband to move back in. I was pulling away from Tom because I was seeing Richard more. Then we planned to go to a family reunion with Richard's family. He left first and told me I should find out how I really felt. So I took his advice literally, and went to see Tom again. When I joined him at the family reunion, I found myself in a beautiful tropical paradise with my husband. But I had to abstain from having sex and had no choice but to tell Richard I had seen Tom again.

Why do you think it is so hard for someone to tell the truth when they are having an affair?

In order to protect it.

Do you feel that there has been no one there to understand your side of the situation?

Yes, I've felt that a lot. I don't know how people go through this and then stay in their marriage. Unless Richard can accept the fact and say, "Yes, it happened. You fell in love with someone else and you are still here," I can never feel close with him again and open up. I have this hidden side of me—this desire, this memory—that I can't expose. How can you truly be in love in a marriage without that trust and openness?

Does Richard feel that the marriage has changed from what it was before?

Yes. He has been in a deep depression. The affair has eroded our trust, but even before, it wasn't a pure, open relationship. We were together, but we didn't have the history we have now, so it was easier to open up and be honest. Then there was nothing to hide.

What would it take for you to feel safe again?

You can't have these experiences with somebody and then forget them. There is so much anger and resentment between Richard and me, it's almost impossible to erase it all. We need to forgive each other for all the pain we have caused. If he could just forgive, let go, and move on, we might be able to get close again. But there's too much stress in everyday life, continuously for over a year and a half.

Then why do you stay in your marriage?

That's a good question. I stay in it though know that in some ways it's a lie. The reasons for staying may seem shallow, but they are good reasons to me. I believe in marriage, but the intimacy and passion are gone. We are very good, old friends who have fun and like to do things together. I don't know if I could have that much fun with anyone but my husband, and I care about him very much as a human being.

What happened between you at the reunion?

Six hours after I met him on the vacation, he wanted to send me back, but I couldn't get a flight. We had planned a fabulous trip, so I said, "Let's just go. It may be our last vacation together. Let's be adult about this, have a good time, and say good-bye."

I can't believe the position I had put myself in, to go 3,000 miles and then tell my husband I had seen my lover. I had no family, no friends, and no money.

We would have fun for a while, and then we would remember what was really happening in our lives and have a fight. On the way home on the plane, he told me, "I'm moving back in. This is going to work or it's over." I had no choice. And that's how it's been ever since. We can't even go out without being nervous that we will run into Tom. I feel like a prisoner.

Now Richard wants to move out of town because he's not happy here anymore, but I am afraid to give up my friends and everything I've worked for, especially if we move to where his family lives because his family knows everything.

Since this all happened, we haven't worn our wedding rings, since he felt we had broken our vows. Now he wants to renew our vows. How can I do that with someone I don't trust and who doesn't trust me?

He has said that if we separate again, it's over. And that's scary, too— my identity is so connected to his. But when I was living alone, I was just beginning to understand who I am. I was happy by myself and realized that I did not need my husband.

Do you feel as though every time you tell the truth, you get punished?
It's not very safe. That's why I feel I can't open up to anyone.

Is it possible that the very thing you are afraid of could be the best thing in the world for you?
It could be. It couldn't be any worse. I feel dragged back down by the fear of being alone. I feel dependent again that I won't be happy unless I am with him, but then I'm not happy now.

Why did you marry him?
I have always looked up to him. When we met, I felt that he was a prize, and I wasn't going to meet very many men like him. I also felt that he would take care of me, and I would be safe. He was handsome and intelligent. I felt lucky, but I always knew that we were very different.

Having once experienced freedom outside your marriage, can you go back to the way you were before?
No, I have changed. I am a different person now and that's a problem for him.

Can you imagine loving him and still following your own path?
Sometimes I don't understand why I am making a big deal out of all this. We don't even have kids. I'm just very attached to him. We've even stopped going to counseling. After a year of trying everything, it just seems futile. Every time it comes to being honest, it doesn't work. I feel there's no hope in resolving this, and then the denial begins.

From all that I have said, it sounds as if I really don't want to be with my husband, but it's still unresolved in my heart. I idealize and dream about what life could be like if only . . . It's hard to let go of my dreams, even if they can never come true.

Do you think this is a dilemma for a lot of women?
A wife wants to be loyal, faithful, honest, and fair. I should have been the one to leave, and when I tried to do it, I was sabotaged. Now it's too painful. I just don't want to go through any more pain. I think society expects women to be martyrs, to sacrifice in order to make things work. I saw that a lot growing up with an alcoholic father.

Is there any way to escape the pain? It seems as though there will be pain, no matter what you do.
My whole life is in limbo right now.

Is this experience a key that will open the door to another way of being, in which you will have power over your own life?
I am hoping that my life will not always be this way. I tried to have the courage to tell the truth, to be honest about what I felt, but that was not acceptable. Having an affair has changed me and continues to do so. I need to find another way of being that works.

And how will you make those changes?
I don't know. It will be good for a few days and then it's awful. Now we are at the point where we have no tolerance for each other's problems or emotions. I can't live my life feeling guilty or pretending to love him. When I see him depressed, it makes me feel like walking away. It's not my fault anymore.

Do you think that things will ever change?
The only option I see is to leave, but that seems harsh, and it makes me question what I have been doing with my life. Being alone cannot be worse than being in a bad relationship. It's a nightmare, but it's hard to change all the cultural conditioning that comes along with it. It's like trying to swim against the tide.

Love as a Drug

Philip was married twice, and both his marriages were disrupted because of affairs with other women. To him, sex was a drug, a high he lived for. In order to heal his sex addiction, Philip embarked on a path of personal therapy and conscious abstinence.

Philip

Do you think people use sex as a drug?

Sex has served as a drug for me. It has helped me numb my feelings of deep loneliness and deep hurt, feelings left over from childhood. Just as you need to continue using a drug, I needed to keep consuming women. There were never enough. And sex was never really satisfying—I always hungered for more.

How did your affairs usually take place?

When I would meet a woman I was attracted to, there was an initial flirtation, which then led to rather lustful play and courtship, which would eventually result in lovemaking and an ecstatic high. After the high of being so spiritually and physically intimate, I would withdraw completely. A hollow feeling would come back inside me. Lovemaking is very intense but offers only a temporary release from that inner void. The woman would usually feel my distance and say something like, "But I thought you were different. I didn't think you were that kind of man." Her feeling of betrayal and disappointment would make me feel even worse, so I would leave and go on to the next one. My life was a vicious cycle.

Did you feel that having affairs was wrong?

Because of the numbness, it was difficult for my inner soul to have much influence whatsoever. I knew that what I was doing was inappropriate, especially if both of us were married to other people. When a secret rendezvous became necessary, I knew it was wrong, but there was excitement and suspense in it. Sometimes, one of our spouses would even be in the same house, and we would sneak off to a private place. The feeling of fear, of being discovered, was always there.

Can you describe the high you got from having affairs?

There was an adrenaline high both from the sexual conquest and the fear of getting caught. It was the same feeling I felt as a boy when my mother sexually molested me. It reinforced the message from the past that I was inherently bad.

Conquest was a big part of it; it's a very macho thing to conquer women. I used to pull back from that stereotype, but that's exactly what I was doing. Conquering means that someone submits to you, and there is a tremendous ego boost in that, especially if a man has low self-esteem.

Do you think that this is typical behavior in men when they initiate sexual relationships with women?

I think that most of us have never known real intimacy with a woman. Most of us were never taught how courtship occurs. No one really told us about sex, so we learned from each other in places like locker rooms in junior high. Some of us explored sex and romance spontaneously, while others waited to have intercourse until we were married. Most of us were not really sure what to do, or how to treat the woman we loved.

I think that the vast majority of men feel this way. You can see it in the way we objectify women. To us, women are incredibly mystifying. Biologically, we seem so different from each other. There's also the subconscious identification with our mother, who was the other significant female in our lives. Most of us were born through a vagina, and ever since we try to get back inside that beautiful, protected, warm, and liquid place. The closest we can get is through our penis.

Why does a man all of a sudden become afraid of a woman and want to leave after making love to her?

He doesn't want any commitments or responsibilities. That's why it was so nice to be able to say I was married, a great excuse if I was having an affair with someone and wanted to get out of it. But sometimes even that didn't work. There were some women who still pursued me even when they knew I was married. They would go to a lot of trouble to set up the next rendezvous. They were just as caught up in the sex and love addiction syndrome as I was.

How have affairs affected your marriage?

I have been married twice to women who really loved me. And considering the state of my self-esteem, I didn't quite understand what that deep kind of love meant. My first wife accepted my actions because of her low self-esteem, but my second wife was not willing to accept them.

I was really committed to my first wife, Andrea, and thought I was in love with her. She was loving, devoted, and monogamous. About a year after we were married, I was taking a walk at the beach on the way home and met a woman who was attracted to me. We talked a while and ended up making love right there in a secluded spot. I think she was horny, so I responded to the natural male instinct to satisfy her need. It was fun. I called her a couple of times later, but she never responded.

I felt guilty about that, but then it got easier. I was always meeting women who were attracted to me, and I must have been putting out that message on some level. Sometimes these women would even come and stay as guests in our home, and I would make love to them there. Completely caught up in my numbness, I was oblivious as to how it would affect Andrea.

When Andrea confronted me after finding a woman's scarf in my car, she said, "I know that you are having affairs. Just don't fall in love." I took that to mean she was giving me permission to continue having affairs. So, I went on doing it. In retrospect, it made me feel that she wasn't strong enough to take a stand, which would have helped me deal with my problem a lot earlier. But I probably wasn't at a point in my life where I was capable of dealing with it. It would have just ended the marriage sooner.

How did the situation come to a crisis?

The marriage itself wasn't working very well. Andrea began getting stronger. She fell in love with a man named Adam, but sexually she was loyal to me, and totally honest about her feelings for him.

Andrea finally found a person who was willing to communicate and be in a healthy relationship with her. For a while, she wanted to have both of us, but I finally said that I couldn't live with it and moved out. She was in love with me for years after that, coming by to visit, sometimes alone and sometimes with her boyfriend. She still would not let go. I cut it off because I couldn't handle the pain of seeing her needs fulfilled by Adam. In my mind, it was okay for me to do that but not her.

I didn't deal with problems very well. It was just what I had done as a child. When something unpleasant happened, I would go in my room and lock the door. It was a way of protecting myself and surviving. I never learned the adult skills of communication and problem solving.

It's ironic that Andrea left you for another man. How did that make you feel?

It was a pattern for me to play the martyr as a survival strategy I learned from childhood. If another man came into the picture, I would typically leave and say, "You are probably better off with him anyway." I never really had the courage or self-esteem to take a stand. I did meet Adam once in an attempt to work things out. I asked him to step aside, and begrudgingly he agreed. When Andrea found out, she was furious and said I had no right to make decisions about her life. I moved out a week later.

I knew I needed to do a lot of work on myself before I was ready for another relationship. I also believed that her leaving me for someone else was somehow my karma, that I was getting paid back for what I had done to her. I really fell apart, almost lost my job, and got very ill. It was a very low point in my life. It reinforced the belief that I couldn't trust women, and that deep inside I must be a very bad person.

Were you able to initiate any new relationships after that?
I no longer pursued women. I dated here and there, but I made love only if they insisted. It was a very painful time for me. I felt very confused. Then I found a nice woman who was a good friend to me. During her marriage, she had lovers, too. So she understood that side of me. But there was also a side of me that didn't want to be with someone who might have affairs. Maybe she would have been faithful, but I will never know.

After your first experience, why did you get married again?
I didn't want to marry Elaine. I just wanted us to live together for a while, but there was tremendous pressure from her family for us to get married. She was in love with me, but she didn't know my dark side and, once it came out, she couldn't deal with it. She had never lived with a man before, nor had she ever had a long-term, committed relationship.

When you went into your second marriage, did you feel that you weren't going to repeat the same pattern?
There were six years between my two marriages, and a lot of growth took place in that time. During my second marriage to Elaine, there have been far fewer affairs—only two or three. And the only reason I had any affairs at all was out of the need for sexual gratification. My sexual needs weren't being met, and the sex addiction was also going on. The women I got involved with were extremely pushy and demanded my participation. All three women pursued me, but only one was attractive to me. We were basically serving each other's sexual needs until the guilt got to be too much.

Until I am fully able to control my sex and love addiction, I need to avoid certain kinds of women. It is my responsibility, not theirs.

What is your status with Elaine now?
We are not living together until we can resolve some of these issues. Our marriage wasn't working, so we separated a year ago. We didn't communicate well, and we were both very unhappy. Based on her upbringing, she expected me to be someone I wasn't, and I was similarly misled. We didn't really take the time to get to know each other before getting married.

How have you dealt with your sex addiction in this marriage?
Sex and love addiction is more than just having intercourse. It is an attitude called "being on the make." Any woman you see is someone you may

potentially seduce, even though you may choose not seduce her. It's an element that involves eye contact, flirting, and being physically close. I was still doing those things but thought I had it under control since I wasn't taking it all the way. Sometimes a man will go to an event with his wife, but not really be with her. He will be with every other woman in the room. I thought my sex addiction had been broken, but it wasn't true. On a subtle level, it was still going on. Finally, I can have eye contact with a woman without that scary feeling that it's going to lead to an affair. I can fantasize, but I don't take it any further. I know my boundaries now, whereas I didn't know them before. My mother didn't know them. I think my sex addiction grew out of being sexually violated by my mother as a child.

Do you want to be monogamous?
I do, and I am not totally sure why. I am not convinced that it is possible, but I would like to try and see what it is like. I have never been totally in love with anyone. It's too scary for me.

Would you describe yourself as a monogamous person?
Now I am.

How did this change take place?
I needed to find within myself the man I professed to be—to be that person rather than just talk about it.

If I am going into a monogamous marriage, it requires making adult decisions when temptation arises. Before, my life was run by an inner teenager who just wanted everything all the time, who lived for immediate gratification. This is a process a lot of men go through in their mid-thirties and forties. Some call it mid-life crisis. I think the process of maturing into adult manhood is a lot more than the typical macho model, nor is it what some people call the soft male.

Was there a particular crisis or event that woke you up?
There was a series of different things. I realized that I might get killed. One jealous husband made a threat against me that really shook me up enough to make me wake up and deal with what I was doing. I finally said no to the woman and had to repeat it to her several times because she kept coming back to me, in spite of her husband's threats, endangering both of us. She had an addiction, too.

I was in my late thirties, in a state of crisis. I knew that something was wrong with me and I wanted to find out what it was. That was when my memories of childhood abuse started surfacing in therapy. I had to admit that I was the person who was responsible for creating the situation with this woman and her husband. So I began to take responsibility, and I began to change.

Has this change in attitude improved your relationship with Elaine?

I think it has. I admitted everything to her, every flirtation I have ever had, everything I have ever done. She encouraged me to share it all, even though it was very painful for her to hear. She said she knew something was going on, though she didn't know specifically who the women were. To me it was a relief.

We are trying to reestablish the trust between us, and that is going to take time, but I am trustworthy now. Whatever happened in the past no longer applies. In the past, I couldn't live with myself because of all the lies. But now I can. I am a lot less confused, I know how to avoid those dangerous situations, and I am really testing myself, but it takes time.

I have friendships with men, and I have friendships with women on a non-sexual basis. I explain to my women friends exactly where I am coming from, so that things are clear right from the start. I am in control of what I do, and I like myself so much more now, I don't need to undermine myself. I am worthy of love, and I am worthy of happiness. I am worthy of success and creativity.

That's what it's all about. I want to be with people who love and support me, regardless of their gender, and I do not choose to be with people who don't.

Do you think that two people can outgrow each other?

Sometimes there is an incubation period when one partner is growing at a faster rate than the other. Growth can happen for one partner or for both. I am growing very fast, and I have invested a lot of time, money, and energy into that process. I feel that if I can do it, anyone can. I think Elaine can grow if she wants to, although I am not one hundred percent sure. Sometimes I have doubts, but I haven't given up on her. I have never really taken a relationship full cycle—I have always just bailed out—so, I want to see this one all the way through.

Has Elaine been able to appreciate and accept your growth?

Yes and no. Because of the pain, it has been very difficult for her to trust me. If the situation were reversed, it would be very hard for me to trust her.

She doesn't have the same confidence in professional therapy as I do. She has gone to a marriage counselor, but hasn't really invested herself in therapy. I have encouraged her to join me, but so far she has resisted it, denying that it's something she needs. When I was so immersed in my own addictions, I couldn't see her for who she was. Now I can look at her differently, and I can see where she needs to change, too. For so long, I perceived myself as the only one with the problems. I was so screwed up, I believed it.

I don't think she really understands the degree of commitment it takes to do this kind of work. It's more than just acknowledging it intellectually. She has her own issues to work on, and it will be interesting to see where she goes with this process.

What do you need in a committed relationship?
I need a good friend who will support me in whatever I want to pursue. There can be constructive criticism, because that helps me clarify what I want. I also want to be with someone who will share the duties of maintaining a home; I want to be with a woman who will consider having children. I don't want someone who is absent from the house all the time. There has to be a certain amount of time we share together.

I need to be with a partner who accepts my limitations, especially in dealing with her family. Basically, I need someone who will allow me to be who I am and allow me to make my own decisions. Sometimes I like to get wild and crazy, especially when I dance at a party. I need to be with someone who can enjoy that part of me and not criticize me for being immature.

When I ask Elaine to go to workshops with me, sometimes she will say, "I can't do this." But I haven't been able to say, "Well, maybe it's best that you and I part, because I need a partner who will grow with me." That is my next step. It could mean separation or total reconciliation.

Do you feel the need to make amends with the women you have had affairs with in the past?
I am in the process of doing that right now, with almost a half dozen women from my past. We have had some enlightening talks. All of us have grown, in a committed relationship with another person, and we are all moving on. We have learned a great deal from each other. This is a small number of the women I have known, but they are significant.

In the past, several women wrote me letters trying to work out what had happened between us. There was one woman who absolutely insisted upon it. She would call and we would meet so that she could understand what had happened, and I would push her away in my usual way. Then for some reason she called when I was at a point in my life when I was ready to process it, but I wasn't able to tell her that I simply wasn't attracted to her. It takes a lot of courage to tell another person what you really think. Then another woman asked directly, "Why wouldn't you want to be with me?" and I told her why. It's difficult to be that honest. In reality, I shouldn't have had a relationship with some of these women.

How many women have you made love to?
Over a hundred, but most of them were one-night stands. The ones I had deep friendships with are women that I really cared for. There is a spiritual

side of these women that I did bond with. That's why it's important to go back and talk about what happened in the past, even though we have moved on. It's an opportunity to heal and feel better about each other.

Have you reconciled with Andrea?
I tried writing letters and calling her. She says that it has taken her eight years to get over me and that she has moved on. I think it is still too painful for her to be friends with me, but it will eventually happen. Someday, I would like to tell her what I appreciate about her in person.

Does that compulsive side of you still exist?
He's still around, but he doesn't control the situation anymore because he's monitored through my therapy. The needy side of me is like a child who wants things and doesn't consider the consequences. I am referring to the abused and shamed parts of my inner child. That unconscious side of me is the same person who was in my mother when she molested me as a child. During the daytime, my mother was a completely different person, and then at night, something demonic in her would take over. It was really scary.

How has that part of you been exorcised?
Celibacy is part of it. But therapy and deep inner work has been essential, integrating my dark side with the part of me I really like. On the cellular level, I am reprogramming how I think of myself. I do this through meditation, hypnotherapy, and affirmation. I am consciously reconstructing my self-image. Being supported by a group has really helped me.

If you have been abused as a child, you do not think you are very worthy of love, and then you feel justified in abusing other people. It's a self-destructive cycle, totally numbing and desensitizing you to the feelings of others—and yourself, of course.

Has that hunger in you finally been satisfied? Do you think you are cured of your sex addiction?
Yes. I would like to think so. One therapist explained that once you have an addiction, it is always part of you. You just learn how to manage it so it doesn't control your life. You may always be an alcoholic, but it doesn't mean you have to drink.

Do you think you could ever revert to your former ways?
I don't think I can afford to. I am in a more conscious state now, where it is no longer necessary to do these things. I am feeling so good about my life, there's no need for it. I can find intimacy with women in other ways. I am part of a group where I feel satisfied by being touched, held, listened to, and enjoyed in a safe environment without any sex. I can now get my personal

needs met in a more appropriate way. I know my strengths and weaknesses, and I know how to move through them without getting stuck.

Now that you have been through so much therapy, what do you think of other people who have affairs?

People do things because they need to, but that doesn't make it right. Having an affair means that you have a need that isn't being fulfilled; there's something lacking in your life, and until you find out what it is, the cycle will continue. I don't condone having affairs, but I really don't want to judge anyone for it. For me, it is inappropriate behavior, but it's not up to me to tell someone else what to do. If someone asks though, I'll advise them to stop.

Do you think that having an affair can be a liberating experience?

All my affairs led me to my liberation. I don't regret what I have done. There are some choices I wish I had made differently, but I have no regrets. I understand now why the events of my life unfolded as they did. I feel at peace with myself. I am looking forward to reaping the harvest of my life work.

Do you feel that you exploited women?

Although in the past I may have abused and betrayed women, I was exploited by them too. We both had basic human needs.

How do you relate to women now?

I can relate to women in a much healthier way now. I really haven't given anything up. There is less sex, but that leaves my energy free for other things. It's still a challenge for me. I still fantasize about women, but we have the right to think anything we want. I want to feel that it's safe to do anything with a woman that I can do with a man. I use that as a barometer. That way I don't feel guilty when I tell my wife that I went for a walk with another woman. I still have a lot of women friends.

Do you feel capable of having a deep, loving relationship now?

I have experienced that kind of love, but I always sabotaged it because it was something I didn't think I deserved. I also had a barrier to intimacy because of my fear of responsibility. I'm at the doorway now. It's possible for me.

Why were you afraid of responsibility?

I was afraid of being trapped by responsibility. It could be a memory of the anxiety and terror left over from childhood.

Do you think that people have a right to include lovemaking as a part of intimacy and sharing?

When it is appropriate. Two people can be out in the woods, sharing a special moment, and lovemaking may be part of that, but when you leave the woods and go home to your own separate lives and commitments, you are responsible for how your actions affect others, and that's what true responsibility is.

As you get healthier and look at the rest of the world, how do you see the quality of most marriages?
Not very healthy. It's difficult since the majority of people in marriages were raised in dysfunctional families so they don't have any idea what a healthy relationship is. They don't see it on television and they don't see it in the movies. There is a small percentage who were raised with good communication skills. They can express their feelings and know how to trust each other. You can trust if you were trusted as a child. I haven't seen too many of these relationships, but I know they exist. Those are the people I want to be around. As I get heathier, I think I will attract the kind of people who are not controlled by their addictions.

What do you think of the institution of marriage?
I think that there is a need for classes in how to be married. People need to be taught how to communicate, how to handle disagreements and feelings—that sort of thing. Most people don't learn these skills in their families, so the dysfunctional patterns just continue. But there's hope.

Do you think that men are changing?
Yes. We may be at the infant stage of personal growth, but we are on the way. More men are joining the men's movement every day, and it is something I am proud to be a part of. Men are now willing to work on themselves, and women are applauding it.

How has the age of AIDS affected your attitude toward having affairs? Is one partner obligated to tell the other if sexual contact has taken place outside the relationship?
There is only one answer to that. If you have any integrity whatsoever, you must tell your partner if you are having an affair. It's a whole new ball game. It's no longer a matter of having a secret little fling; it's a downright flirtation with death.

It's about time—AIDS or not—for men and women to say, "The generational malaise stops here and now." It's a two-way street. Men and women are out there devouring each other, and I was one of those people doing it. They can go on without me.

Aphrodite Is Out of the Closet

As a radical feminist therapist, Naomi saw marriage as a narrow and confining closet, yet she wanted to have children. So she married a suitable partner, had a baby, and lived the usual suburban life for eight years. Suffocated by the mediocrity of her existence and the conventional expectations of her husband, Naomi began having affairs with men she found more stimulating. After juggling her affairs and family life for a period of time, she finally made a decision about the way she wanted to spend the rest of her life.

Naomi

How would you describe the goddess Aphrodite, and what would be the consequences of letting her out of the closet? How would this compare to the myth of Pandora's Box?

Aphrodite, known as Venus to the Romans, is the goddess of love who causes problems in the lives of mortals. When she sends her son Eros (or Cupid) into someone's life, it usually means big trouble. Even the way Aphrodite was born was scandalous. When Kronos castrated his father, Uranus, he threw his testicles into the ocean. The semen mixed with the saltwater and Aphrodite was born on the foam of the sea.

The ancients thought love was a disease. In ancient texts love is Eros— a power so overwhelming that it was often considered an illness like the flu. If you contracted this illness, you were overcome with the desire to surrender to it.

Do you think women were feared?

The Greeks were fascinated by love, yet they also feared it. Women appear in classical literature, but they are usually idealized and put on a pedestal, often a way of dealing with something feared.

According to Hesiod, Zeus created women as punishment because Prometheus dared to bring men fire. Women were thus created out of revenge and Pandora gets blamed for the evils of the world, when it was Zeus who really set her up. Zeus sent Pandora to tempt Prometheus, who sensed the plot and resisted her. When Prometheus' brother, Epimetheus, fell in love with Pandora, he persuaded her to open the box. What happened was a mutual decision, yet she takes the blame. This is similar to the Adam and Eve story; Eve gets blamed for causing the sins of the world.

Would you say that in antiquity women were regarded as inferior to men and treated as second-class citizens?

Definitely. Aristotle said that women are deformed males.

And the love and passion that women inspire in men were considered more dangerous than the bloodiest war?

Although Greece was the basis for western civilization, the Greeks shouldn't be idealized. You have to remember that all of classical Greek literature describes only the top five percent of the elite. The common people were not represented.

Men were expected to marry in order to procreate, but the preferred form of sexuality among the privileged was homosexuality. Homosexual relationships between equals were forbidden. What *was* considered normal for a man was to marry and have affairs on the side either with prostitutes, who were the only women with any kind of freedom, or young boys. A wife stayed at home indoors except for funerals and two festivals a year with her servants doing all the errands for her.

The Greeks and Romans were very much like us. Women had love affairs. I have read the transcript in Greek of the trial of a man who killed his wife's lover. He was going to be freed because adultery was considered highly immoral and therefore his action was justified. A lot of people had affairs, but nobody talked about it, just like today. The laws were instituted to protect the family.

You have to realize that the literature of those times served the same purpose as movies in our culture. It was written to be sensational and entertaining and certainly was not a reflection of everyday life. Imagine if a society two thousand years from now watched a movie made in 1992 and thought that represented everyday life in our times.

Did women have lesbian relationships?

Probably. All we have are the writings of Sappho, a Greek woman who wrote to her lesbian lover in the sixth century B.C. There are some references to women being intimate in the comedies of Aristophanes, but there is nothing explicit.

Do you think that the metaphor of Pandora's Box applies to our contemporary society?

I believe that many of us interact on a subliminal level. I have what I call the ducky theory, based on the idea that ducks and other animals bond to the first thing they see as their primary source of love. There's a classic children's story in which a duck sees a tractor and thinks it's his mother. We think we grow up, become adults, and distance ourselves from those primal responses. We think we are independent and capable of making logical choices, but it's often the ducky inside of us that bonds with that memory of what we remember as our primary source of love. These attachments go so far back from a time before we learned logic and language. That's why people will fall in love with a fantasy, why they feel so compelled and confused. That's why people feel a tremendous desire to be with someone when it doesn't make any sense. And that's why, at times, an affair seems so magical—it's really coming from a child's way of thinking.

Isn't it good for people to get in touch with their intuitions to balance the usual emphasis on the logical?
The mistakes I have made in my past and mistakes that I have seen other people make are often based on these intuitive feelings. However, sometimes they are positive and sometimes they are negative intuitions. Sometimes a person looks right because it's familiar, not because it's really right. So you dive in and get involved without really finding out enough about the person, nor do you understand what's driving you so that you can take the time to determine what's healthy and what's not. Intuition has to be weighed against firsthand experience.

You have to ask yourself, is this person a good person, is he or she committed to being a healthy individual, is he or she helping me to grow, or am I simply repeating my past? You inevitably get to face many of these questions in a long-term relationship, but in the short-term affair, because it is so volatile, you often get to learn only in retrospect.

Do you think people are drawn to each other out of karma or destiny?
I go both ways on this one. The first time I saw my husband, Luke, I said, "I am going to marry this man." There is no reason why I should have had this thought; I don't know where it came from, but I will never forget it, because it was so intense. We got to know each other, started a relationship, and within a year and a half, I married him. Some people would call it subliminal recognition; others would call it karmic destiny. The psychological approach would be that it wasn't destined or magical, but a subconscious response, maybe even a biological urge to procreate. Perhaps I was just choosing a father for my child.

So, people meet, they marry and mate for logical and illogical reasons. What goes wrong? Why do people have affairs?
I wouldn't say that affairs are symptomatic of anything wrong.

Would you say that an affair is a healthy thing?
It can be. I think it's as healthy as the people who are involved. I think that marriage can be sick as well. Marriages are often the unhealthiest relationships, while affairs can end up bringing the greatest health and

happiness. Whether it's a marriage or a love affair, a relationship is only as heathy as the people who are in it.

Anything that has to happen in isolation has more potential for becoming unhealthy. There's more fertile ground for developing problems, because you don't have the feedback from other people in society. Secrecy breeds shame. So affairs often suffer simply because they have to be kept secret. Everybody in any kind of relationship, whether a marriage, friendship, parenthood, or love affair, needs to be able to talk to other people about it. But people are *not* allowed to discuss affairs. Even if you do, often it's either sensationalized or trivialized. An affair is categorized as taboo, an action that goes against the natural order of society. That is what I would call primitive thinking. None of us are free from it, nor are we free from those around us who think that way.

What kind of person transcends this conditioning?
Nobody.

What is the drive to do something that requires such a great risk?
It's different for each person. Some people take the risk because they are addicted to emotional intensity. Some people can get turned on only by doing something clandestine and can enjoy a sexual relationship only if it's transgressive. But that does not apply to most people. Most people want to be happy and to feel intimate with another person, which, unfortunately, is very difficult to experience. People are willing to take the risk to broaden their own ability to connect with another human being.

Maybe a woman's connection with her husband doesn't include her artistic or playful side, which may be of great importance to her. She can put that part of her nature aside so that her marriage can work, but she still can't deny it. This is why people are compelled to find inner fulfillment and wholeness through relationships with others. Taking the risk is life enhancing; it makes one feel more alive. That's the point of relationships in the first place, to feel more expansive, more connected, and less isolated. The people who have successful outside relationships are willing to be very honest with themselves and are willing to grow.

What about the person who can manage both kinds of relationships simultaneously?
I really don't know anyone who has managed to do that. Most of the people I know who have kept affairs going in their life have managed to turn their affairs into friendships. The primary connection is transformed, the only way they can continue. Or the affairs with sporadic meetings over a long period of time—maybe once or twice a year—but I hesitate to call those liaisons real affairs, they are more a rendezvous or vacation.

What is your opinion of people who have a pattern of having one affair after another as a kind of sex addiction?

I don't like them, I don't trust them. I think that they are very unhealthy and ought to go into therapy. I don't think their affairs have anything to do with intimacy. Probably they are so damaged and so afraid of intimacy that philandering is a substitute. Philandering is an act of anger; it's just a matter of getting laid, and getting laid is no more intimate than rape, which is not an act of sex but an act of aggression. I think philandering hurts the people who do it and the people involved.

What about two people who have outgrown each other? For example, the wife may ask her husband to grow with her, but he denies that there is a problem. Often she will explore these new avenues in a new relationship, typically an affair. Is it best for her to follow her own path and leave the marriage, or should she try to work it out?

That's a very familiar scenario, and it's a real pickle. There is a lot to be lost and gained with both choices. I was brought up in a family where women always sacrificed for their families. Always. Women were only educated so that they could support themselves and their children if their husbands were incapacitated. Education for women was also important in the upper class as a social skill; women needed to be able to talk intelligently at dinner parties. So my early training was to stay in the family, deny the love affair, and compromise myself, and maybe I would take up watercolor painting to channel the energy in a safe way that wouldn't threaten the status quo.

My mother ended up dying at the age of fifty-eight, and I think she died of boredom. Her kids grew up and there was nothing for her to do. It's sad because she was extremely talented and creative, but without any education. My father, a brilliant doctor, could have gone on forever. It has been my experience that the woman who makes choices similar to my mother's harbors great resentment. You don't feel holy and wonderful about yourself in your martyrdom, because what you are sacrificing is yourself, and you end up hating the other person for it. You may do it because you love the person, but you hate that person at the same time, and then you begin to hate yourself. It is a downward spiral into depression and despair. You can't hold another person responsible for making you happy. You are the only one who can do that. Ultimately, your happiness is your own responsibility.

How did your mother's experience affect you as a young woman? Were you determined not to end up like her?

Absolutely. The way that I have designed my life differently is to be honest—to be honest with myself about what I want in my life that will make me happy so that I don't end up blaming somebody for my own unhappiness. I don't want to make a choice and then say to someone, "I made this choice because of you."

The first time I left my husband Luke, I moved into a little cabin on my professor's property. I was just finishing my senior thesis at the time. Luke was so resentful that I was finishing college that living with him had become physically abusive. So there I was on my own for the first time. I remember shopping for groceries and pushing the cart around the store for about an hour. I had been cooking and buying groceries for my family for so long that I honestly couldn't remember what I liked to eat. After an hour and a half, I ended up with some diet Pepsi and yogurt. I went home and sobbed.

This was after I had already been in therapy for some time—long enough to make the break with Luke. I had to rediscover how to stock my refrigerator and cook for myself. Now I know what I love to eat. I constantly have to ask myself in each situation: What do *I* want? For years I haven't had permission to exercise my choice. I have had to retrain myself to know what I want to do.

When you were married and got involved in an affair, how did it affect your marriage?

Maybe I should go back to the beginning, to my first affair. When I first met Luke, we lived together for the first year or so. He had so many qualities that I liked. We lived in a house that he had built. He was a well-educated professional, and we were great friends.

We got married, and he changed almost instantly. The roles became different. As his wife, I was supposed to defer to him, whereas before we had been equals. And the sex wasn't as good. He paid less attention to me physically and emotionally immediately after marriage. He became more controlling about where I went, whom I spoke to, and what I did. I wanted a divorce six months after I got married. I knew it was a mistake.

Why do you think marriage does this to people?

Conditioning. People imitate how Mom and Dad were when they got married. Marriage partners are like business partners, and it's normal to model your life after your parents'. I know how Luke's parents were with each other, and that's very much how he treated me.

My first affair was with a woman. Talk about letting Aphrodite out of the closet! The idea of being involved with a woman had never even crossed my mind. I was making a delivery to San Francisco with a woman who worked with me, and it meant spending the night there. We ended up making love, and I was shocked at how wonderful it was. I can remember driving home with her the next day; I couldn't believe what had happened. It didn't seem wrong; it seemed that we had become more intimate. We had expressed our love for each other. We had definitely opened Pandora's Box, but I refused to feel ashamed, and I was not going to keep it a secret.

So I told Luke about it, and the shit hit the fan. He told his parents, he told all our friends, he did everything he could to embarrass me, but I still refused to conform to what he wanted. I made him move out and continued my relationship with Alison for six months. I felt betrayed by the way Luke had changed in our marriage. Before we were married, my relationship with Alison would have been acceptable. Now it was a crisis. At the end of six months, I decided that my family was more important than my sexual freedom. So, I went back to Luke.

What was it like putting Aphrodite back in the closet?
It was really sad, because I felt that Luke couldn't accept who I was. So I had to conform to his way of doing things, pretending to be a certain way so that he would be happy. I accommodated him.

Just after my affair with Alison, Luke and I got back together in a very strong way. We increased our commitment to each other and worked through a lot of the issues about marriage; we went to couples' counseling and decided to have a baby together. We grew a lot during those years.

Before I got pregnant, I went on a vacation alone to New Mexico for a month. That's where I met José. We had a brief but delightful affair. I didn't think much of it. Then I returned home, and I got pregnant.

After our son was born, another change took place. My mother died when Jimmy was one year old. Luke's way of dealing with my mother's death was to tell me to go in the bedroom and close the door because my crying upset him. Both Luke and his parents took the attitude: "It's just as well."

From the time Jimmy was born, Luke's *modus operandi* was to feel burdened by a family he had to support. To him, I was even more of a liability because I was the mother and he had to become the primary provider. The truth is that I was miserable at home with this baby. I really wanted to do something, to produce something.

Three nights a week, I led therapy groups, working with issues around rape and domestic violence, but counseling is more like parenting than friendship. During the day, I sat in the house with my little baby while Luke was off doing his art. I was starved for conversation and friendship. That's when I would call José who became one of my dearest friends. I could talk to him about anything.

When Luke came home, there was nothing to talk about; we had no shared experience. And he had no ambition for improving our lifestyle. I wanted to move into a nicer house, and he wanted to move back to a cabin in the woods where he didn't have to pay any rent, a cabin with no running water and no plumbing. He was furious that I had made him upgrade. He wouldn't pay the bills until the red notices came in, then he would squeak out a few bucks. It wasn't that he didn't make the money; it was a way of controlling me. Meanwhile, I was stuck at home breast-feeding a three month old. It was like being held hostage.

How did you break out of that?

It took a long time. Luke was my abuser, in a sense, because it really was like living in captivity. Yet he was also my comfort and the person I was closest to. He was the person I had given my body to in the process of having a child.

My father died a year after my mother, and then my best friend died of cancer. I couldn't get any comfort or support from Luke, but to this day José is a pillar of support, and I have grown to love him. I never wanted to leave Luke for him, but the intimacy and love between us is something I can count on.

When my parents died, I went through a period of tremendous despair. A therapist friend made the comment that I wasn't unhappy because of the grief, but because my marriage was so horrible. She felt that Luke was contributing nothing to the relationship. I felt like I did seventy-five percent of the work, emotionally, physically, and financially. Yet I still really needed his twenty-five percent. So I made a five-year plan—my strategy for getting out of my marriage. I knew that I had to depend on Luke for five years, until Jimmy was in school. So, I went back to school to get the education I needed to start a new career. I knew I did not want to stay in the role of a therapist. I was sick of psychology and wanted to something in the realm of academic scholarship, so I chose the classics.

Were there other affairs?

Yes. I got involved with a teacher at the college where I was taking classes. We were close in age, and very much equals. It wasn't the classic professor/student twenty-five-year gap. Dan was married and had children. I knew it was never going to be anything more than an affair, but because I was experiencing so much grief and unhappiness, I wanted to do something that would make me feel good, that would make me feel alive. It was fantastic. Dan and I waited until the semester was over, so that we would not be vulnerable to campus gossip or breaking any sexual harassment laws. As wonderful as the affair was, it was also very painful because it represented everything that I didn't have at home with Luke: fun, laughter, good sex, being taken seriously as an intellectual. My marriage reminded me of a quote by Marilyn French from *The Women's Room*: "Marriage is lonelier than solitude."

I loved being with Dan and missed him terribly when he left to go on sabbatical in the fall. Then I got involved in my second affair with a man who lived three thousand miles away. We met at a cocktail party while I was visiting a friend on the East Coast. He was an Ivy League professor, about twenty years my senior and also married. He was a very prestigious and accomplished author, fluent in many languages, and well traveled. An extremely interesting intellectual and talented artist, he stimulated me in so many ways.

We even went to Europe together, unbeknown to my husband or to anybody. We spent a month traveling together. I did very little to hide what was going on. My husband knew so little about me that he didn't know about any of these affairs.

Did you have to lie?
I had to lie, but I never had to lie about the affairs. He never actually asked me point-blank: "Are you having an affair?" I just told him I was going to Europe on business. He was more upset that I was spending money than anything else.

Did you give yourself permission to have these affairs out of defiance for his neglect?
I felt very committed to staying in the marriage, maybe for the wrong reasons. I was doing it for my children. I love my husband. I love him to this day, and I don't want to hurt him. I felt guilty that I might hurt him, but I was making a choice of the lesser of two evils. I could choose to stay in the marriage, not have the affairs, be miserable and resentful, grow old and die, without ever being able to feel what I wanted to feel—or I could have the affairs, feel guilty, and at the same time feel excruciatingly alive. Of course, my affairs were not always sheer pleasure; they were often filled with angst.

Would you say that the affairs were a matter of survival?
Yes, I felt as though I was drowning in a sea of despair. Parenting was really the only thing that held Luke and me together.

Did you fear that if your marriage failed, it would be a reflection on you?
Yes, I did. I didn't want to get married again. I didn't want to be a single woman looking for a partner. A lot of times I would negate my own feelings of unhappiness, thinking: "Maybe I'm just too demanding. Maybe I'm the kind of person that nobody could ever make happy."

Did you feel you were entitled to have these affairs in order to make yourself happy? Or did you feel guilty?
I did care what people thought, and I always felt guilty, but I needed to know that life was worth living, and what makes life worth living for me is love and connectedness. I felt I deserved these experiences, and I felt grateful and blessed for them. I felt that there was a God, and that I was being taken care of, even though I was living in a state of spiritual famine. I was getting the nurturing I needed. I knew I was going to have to break some rules to keep from starving to death, but it was worth it.

Did any of your lovers want you to leave your husband?

Yes, the last one, and that relationship was the most difficult. After that one, I never wanted to be involved in another affair again. I have a very large container of pain, and up until then my despair had been contained. This person was actually available; he wasn't married. He was fun, intellectual, and ten years younger than I. He loved me in a passionate, emotional way. It was a very intense and not particularly healthy relationship, because of the isolation and secrecy. He became good friends with my kids and wanted me to leave Luke. He was going to graduate school and wanted me to go with him, but it was absolutely implausible. He was a young grad student with no income, and I had plans for my own graduate education in a different school. Ending the affair was incredibly painful. We had bonded more than I had with anyone else, and the sex was always so good.

Had you envisioned a future with any of the other men you had been involved with?

Only in fantasy, never in reality, but I did with this one.

What happened after that?

I ended up leaving my husband and went into a period of seclusion. I spent the next year separated from Luke, living in the cabin, finishing my degree. I needed time to sort things out. I got very involved with therapy, remembering events from my childhood which I hadn't remembered before. I began to focus on myself and my own academic goals. It was nice *not* to be in a relationship with anyone, and I made a commitment not to get involved with anyone else while I was married. Although my past affairs allowed me to experience the goodness of life, they kept me from confronting the dissatisfaction within myself. I knew that phase of my life had passed.

Were the affairs as much of a distraction as they were a catalyst for growth?

Nobody should make you feel that good, and nobody should make you feel that bad. To me that was an indication that there was something wrong— something I needed to understand the cause of. I had to stop the pattern of allowing relationships to be my primary focus and my source of pain.

For a long time, I thought it was just the affairs, and the marriage somehow existed in a separate realm. I thought the affairs were the charming dirt roads of my existence, full of beautiful scenery, and my marriage was the highway of my life. After I stopped having affairs, I discovered that the highway was no different from the dirt roads. My relationship with Luke was just as torturous, requiring constant negotiation. I realized that I needed to stop and listen to what was going on inside of me. And that's what I have been trying to do. It's very hard and also very rewarding to be alone. At first, it was incredibly difficult. There were a lot of voices inside me crying out for things that I didn't feel, needs that were not going to be met. All I had to do was listen to the voices; I didn't have to meet all those needs. Then it became rewarding. Those voices took me deeper inside myself, where I discovered what existed inside of me. It can be expressed outwardly, but it lives inside. I have found it extremely exciting to realize that I have an impermeable boundary around myself and that I don't have to let anybody in. I don't have to give myself away in order to feel connected. I can feel connected just with myself. And if I choose to let someone inside my boundaries, it can be extremely rewarding, but it is not essential.

How have you reconciled your marriage in light of all this growth and understanding?

I have chosen to end my marriage after a series of events which made it obvious that we needed to split up. Yet I still feel a lot of grief and there are still times when I miss Luke very much. Although I feel sad, I do feel better now. I have worked through the initial guilt and am now in more of the depressed phase. I have to be careful not to initiate any new bonds at this time, because I feel that it's too soon, it would be a mistake. That's hard for me, because I also believe that if God sends someone into your life to share things with, it's a blasphemy not to accept the gift of love.

Is it a relief to know that your marriage is not ending because of the affairs you had?

The reason why I always went back to Luke was out of guilt. Now I was able to admit that I just wanted out of the marriage. Period. No drama was necessary.

I feel convinced that I gave my marriage its best shot. During the past three years, when I was not having any affairs, I worked damn hard to be as honest and authentic, as open and as caring as I possibly could be, and things never really got better. I don't think that Luke knows me. He knows who he wants me to be, but he hasn't ever really known *me*.

Do you think you will ever experience a relationship with someone who truly knows you?

I would like to be able to answer yes to that, but I think that may not be. Not that I am a cynic; I really would like to find the right person. But in reality, the world is not kind to older women. The standards of youth and beauty are so high that once a woman reaches forty, the chances of it happening are slim. I am not going to live my life in search of it. My life is on the brink of blossoming with things that I have worked very hard for career-wise. I love my work, which brings me great satisfaction. The most wonderful thing I have discovered in the last three years is that I don't need relationships in order to be happy.

If you had it to do all over again, would you do anything differently?

Given what I had to work with, given my family scenario that I grew up in, I think that I have done a remarkable job. I was built to self-destruct. My parents were addicted to prescription drugs. They were dysfunctional with a capital "D." It's a miracle that I have not become an alcoholic or suicidal. That's probably why I chose to be a therapist for so long. Even though I have made some bad choices, I have gotten out of abusive relationships.

If I had it to do over again, I probably would have started my own therapy earlier. That is where I really shortchanged myself. For a long time, I thought that I was the person who didn't need therapy, that I was strong, that I could handle it all with a natural honesty. I needed to do a very deep self-investigation, and establish a bond with a therapist whom I could trust. I wish I had done that sooner.

Do you believe that our future is dictated by our past?

You can't remove your history but you can examine your life. Some people don't need to examine themselves—they can live very happily the way they are. That just wasn't the case for me.

Is Aphrodite alive and well in your life?

Aphrodite is thriving. She is alive and well, and loves good sex. She's a wild woman. In my life, Aphrodite needs to be bridled, but I will never put her back in the closet again. Aphrodite is a source of great pleasure, and she makes life worth living.

What is your advice to someone who is in the midst of an affair?

Find someone who is wise that you can talk to about it. Human intimacy deserves the best. If you are in an affair, you might as well make it work for you.

Is having an affair a curse or a blessing?

I think that it is a blessing. If two people can love each other and walk away leaving each other intact, while maintaining the integrity of everyone involved, an affair can only enhance life. Everyone needs a confidant, someone who will give you support and permission to discover what you really want. And it's usually not what you think it is.

An Honest Woman

Having followed a path of personal growth for many years, Rosalind realized that it was more natural for her to share her life with a woman than a man. She finally made the decision and left her husband whom she loved for another woman. In the following interview, Rosalind speaks candidly about the changes that took place in her life as a result of falling in love with another woman.

Rosalind

What happens when a woman falls in love with another woman?

First of all, I have to say that I have always been more attracted to women than men. These feelings started when I was about fourteen or fifteen, although I didn't do anything about it until I was about twenty-one. For a long time, I chose the straight road even though I had experimented being with women. It took me a long time even to be able to say the word "lesbian." Personally, I don't like to label myself that way—I hate labels. Because of all the stereotyping, it took me a long time to accept the way I am, to give myself permission to live with a woman. I had and still have in some ways a tremendous fear of not being accepted by society.

What are some of the stereotypes and misconceptions about lesbians that you encountered?

I didn't have any positive role models. According to the viewpoint I was raised with, lesbians were unattractive, masculine women. The butch-dyke stereotype of a lesbian was as frightening to me as a big, hefty construction worker who harassed women on the street. Another misconception I ran into was the idea that there is always a male role and a female role in a lesbian relationship. Gender scripting exists in almost any relationship, defining everything from cooking, cleaning, parenting, making money, and paying bills to arranging vacations and taking out the garbage. In today's relationships, those roles are more flexible and equal than they ever have been before. It doesn't matter whether the role is male or female. Lots of women work while their men cook and raise children.

Do you feel that you have to keep the fact that you are a lesbian a secret, just like someone who is having an affair?

I try not to be secretive. If it comes up, I am honest about my life. When I interviewed for my present job, I told my employers that my partner was a woman. I told them that if they had a problem with my lifestyle, they shouldn't hire me. But they did anyway. I am lucky to have found such an open-minded workplace.

Are you ever attracted to men?

Sure, I appreciate men. I have had some good sexual relationships with men. To this day, I can still imagine enjoying sex with men. Some of my fantasies involve men. But there was always a voice inside telling me that I would rather live in the company of a woman—to love her and build my life with her. For a long time I didn't listen to that voice. One day, I met a wonderful man named Martin. We became best friends; we had wonderful communication, great sex, and shared adventures together. We even got married, but inside, that one phrase kept coming up: "You really would rather be with a woman."

What was your relationship with Martin like?

We were together for four years and married for two and a half. Martin knew that I had had sexual relationships with women, and he accepted it, but it wasn't something we talked about.

Our marriage was a normal, happy relationship with all the usual issues. It was very similar to the kind of relationship I have now—having fun, sharing intense discussions about values and politics, talking through problems when they arose. We were very compatible, but inside, I felt incomplete with him. I felt that I was lying to myself about something. I suppose there are many women who live their lives that way—women who have good relationships with their men but wish that their men were women.

What motivated you to leave your marriage?

After four years with Martin, that inner voice became intolerably loud. I met a woman with whom I was very friendly. When I found out she was gay, my interest in her increased rapidly. Jeanette and I were working together on a creative project that was ready to take off. She was beautiful and confident, and what we were working on was very exciting. At the time I was very vulnerable, and I allowed her to seduce me. I was hungry for the kind of attention and excitement she gave me.

Did you have an affair with her?

We had an intellectual affair for several months. I just don't feel good about lying, especially to the person I am committed to. I am also a lousy liar, so I told Martin as soon as I began to have feelings for Jeanette. Being a very open person, he accepted that I needed to explore those feelings, even though he was hurt and scared.

I feel that I owe the truth to my friends and to myself, even if it hurts. I was brought up that way. Honesty has gotten me a lot farther in life than lying. It's a personal code of ethics. I feel good about never having lied to Martin, though it was hard on us both.

Did that mean leaving the relationship?

For a few weeks while I was having my affair with Jeanette I tried to stay with him, but I was falling deeply in love with her. I remember waking up in bed one day with Martin, feeling as though I didn't belong there. I knew I couldn't stay with Martin anymore. I immediately called a therapist and made the decision to leave. That voice inside, that phrase that had been telling me I would rather be with a woman, started to become a reality.

Unfortunately, the relationship with Jeanette didn't last. It was wonderful for several months, but we were both on the rebound from other relationships. As the fire cooled down, we found that the real basis for relationship wasn't there. So we broke it off. I hoped someday to find a relationship with a woman that would be more compatible.

Did you have any regrets later about the decision you made?

Not really. It would have happened sooner or later and I felt so happy and relieved that I was finally being true to myself. Even after I broke up with Jeanette, I enjoyed being alone for several years.

Did you have other relationships with women?

I had a few relationships on and off, especially a very dysfunctional one that lasted a year and a half. Even that was something I needed to go through to be where I am today.

When I was ten years old, my mother had a psychotic breakdown. While I was growing up, becoming a young woman, she just wasn't there for me. As a result, I tended to seek women who were emotionally undependable, like her. It was my role to take care of them and try to solve their problems. It never worked, but somehow their emotional instability seemed to spark something in me.

Do you think that people use affairs to play out dysfunctional patterns?

After my relationship with Jeanette, I realized that I was attracted to what was most familiar, but not always most healthy. I think that's human nature. Naturally, you try to find someone who will feed your subconscious needs. If you find yourself in the same situation again and again, life is trying to tell you something. You are hungry for that same feeling and you meet someone who will feed it, so you think it's love, but it's just a form of love addiction. If you are in the heat of an affair, ask yourself if it doesn't remind you of one you have had before.

Rosalind 63

I developed a visual image to help me: In my right hand I had all my subconscious patterns and a voice that recognized the same incompatible lover who kept reappearing in my life. In my left hand I had information and a voice that said, "This is the kind of person who is not good for me. I'm going to get hurt. It may be hot and fun for a while, but it is going to die. This person is not a friend."

I finally learned how to listen to the voice in my left hand. I am glad I was able to break the pattern of passion and betrayal, and no longer need to work out unresolved issues from my past. It took three more relationships to learn to choose women who were not going to betray me. I finally got some therapy and broke the pattern. Three years ago, I found a wonderful, brilliant partner who is stable and happy like me. We are motivated by the same values and have been able to reach our dreams together.

What does having an affair mean to you?

To me having an affair means doing something that is not honest. It means going outside the relationship you are committed to, at the other person's expense. If you can't find what you need in your relationship, you should communicate your need and work through it, or end the relationship. I do whatever I can to fulfill my needs within my relationship. Sometimes, I simply need to feel free to do something on my own. I think that's one reason why people have affairs. They need to feel free, and they find someone who makes them feel that way.

If you are lying to someone you have agreed not to lie to, you are violating your integrity. If you have agreed to be monogamous in your marriage, why break the agreement? Sexual loyalty should be respected, and sexual intimacy should be shared only with each other—if that is the agreement two people have made.

When one partner goes behind the other's back and shares that sacredness with someone else, that's betrayal. If both people agree *not* to be monogamous, that's fine. You can always change the rules, but you have got to put your cards on the table. I don't care if a person is monogamous or not; I just don't like people who lie.

I have been involved with people who were not monogamous, and I tried to make them monogamous. Every time I failed.

Do you think that having an affair is a symptom that there is something wrong?

I think that lying is a symptom of something wrong in the relationship. On some level, I think that the person who is being lied to knows. The emotional bond between two people is so strong that the other person can usually tell. Lying is what causes the real damage. Having an affair is not immoral, but people need to be honest about what they are really doing.

Why do you think that some people need to lie?

For some it's a survival skill, especially for those who were raised in a situation where lying was the only way to get what they wanted.

Movies and television glorify betrayal and deception. Perhaps this is why it is so hard for people to find standards for a healthy relationship.

People get involved in affairs from an addictive place. It's a high just like a drug. Most of the people are just looking for love.

What about the person who is having an affair in order to get out of an abusive situation?

There are situations when a person needs to do that, and it's really sad. Nevertheless, I still think that it's wrong to make an agreement with someone and break the agreement without letting the other person know. Every time you lie, it robs you of your personal power.

Do you think there are women who love other women because they fear and hate men, especially men who have been abusive, controlling, and exploitative?

Yes, there are, though most of the women I have known in abusive situations seem to stay with that kind of man. I think it's another misconception that most gay women have been abused by men. I know some women who have never been with a man. They were clear about their sexuality at a very young age.

I am in a partnership with a woman because it fits who I am. We don't have a lot of the marital problems our straight friends have: we talk through things easily, we have our own personal finances, we don't have to worry about roles. I tend to do all the cooking because I love to cook.

We even have our own friends. Some we share, some we don't. Some are gay, some are straight. We've never gone to bed angry, although sometimes we have stayed up late to talk. We don't let resentments build up, and we don't inhibit each other's freedom. We know how to ask for what we need. And if it's something the other person can't give, we look inside to see if it's something we can give ourselves. We know that you can't expect to have all your needs fulfilled by one person. That's the value of having good friends.

My personal philosophy requires that I continue reaching for my goals, enriching myself and others, attracting the energy that makes my life better and better. I thank God every day for a wonderful life, a wonderful partner, and a healthy body. I pray that will continue. The thought of living a lie would disease me.

What should a woman do if she is having an affair because she is unhappy in her marriage?

If a woman wakes up one day and realizes that she is trapped, that her marriage has been denying her personal freedom, then she obviously needs to grow. She needs to get help, preferably with her husband, so that they might find ways for the relationship to change. Otherwise she is going to have to leave.

The best way is for her to express her needs and for him to listen. They should try to work it out and if they can't, they should go to counseling. A lot of times that works. If he gets abusive, I hope that she would leave immediately. If he refuses to change, then I hope she would continue her personal growth anyway.

The dynamics of an abusive relationship are the same whether it is straight or gay. If a woman's answer to leaving an abusive man is to get involved with a woman, she could be attracted to an abusive woman. The inner work has to come first. Until you work out your own dysfunctional patterns, it is hard to have healthy relationship with anyone.

Do you think an affair has much of a chance of surviving a long time?
Most of them exist in the realm of fantasy, but I suppose that in some cases they work. I know a woman who has been a mistress to a married man for many years. She has her independence, she doesn't have to do his laundry, and she gets to enjoy the fun part of life with her lover, but she is also very lonely.

Maybe some people have affairs because they don't want a traditional marriage. Some people are afraid of the long-term commitment that marriage implies, and most affairs typically don't last forever. The people just go along for the ride, and when the fun is over, they say good-bye. Then they go on to the next one.

Maybe there's a woman out there reading this book who is having an affair and thinks her husband doesn't know. And maybe he's doing the same thing. If they got together and opened up about what's going on, maybe they could live the rest of their lives happily having affairs now and then. Anything's possible. My ideal would be for one to say to the other, "I am feeling the need to have an affair. So let's go do something wild. Let's meet for lunch and then go to a motel for the afternoon." It might be the most liberating thing in the world.

If you have been having lots of affairs and are unhappy, my advice is to be smart. Make the man use a condom and call a therapist. If you have an infection that won't heal, go to a doctor. So much good help is available today, both individually and in groups. There's no excuse—you can find help if you need it.

What do you think women have to offer each other that men don't?
Men are learning to offer more emotional nurturing than they used to. Women are teaching them, and men are teaching each other. I feel very positive about the men's movement. As men get in touch with their vulner-

ability, and women get in touch with their self-esteem, the quality of relationships will improve. Maybe we can wean ourselves from the need to rely on gender scripting and labels.

Who is your role model?
Katharine Hepburn. Whenever I am faced with a difficult and vulnerable situation, I ask myself, "Now what would Kate Hepburn do?"

How do you deal with the myth that a woman needs a man to be complete?
Some women need women, and some women need men. Ten percent of our society is gay. I feel complete unto myself, but it's much nicer to be with a partner. People tend to be happier, live longer, and have less disease when they are in a good partnership. This is the healthiest relationship I have ever had, one that I have worked hard to be capable of.

What are the characteristics of a healthy relationship, gay or straight?
Mutual respect, excellent communication, and good health. Successful problem solving is also important and knowing when to get help. And being best friends. Relationships come in all different shapes and sizes. There are some great relationships that don't include sex.

How do you deal with our society's homophobia?
I don't make gestures of affection in public, because I don't want to invite dirty looks. Even in a straight relationship, I wouldn't feel comfortable kissing in public.
For the most part, it's society's problem. A lot of that fear and hatred comes from indoctrination and ignorance, and the tendency to harass a minority. It all comes back to fear—many people who hate gay people have never known a gay person.

Do you think that there is a tendency among gays toward promiscuity? To what degree is AIDS a concern?
Once again, that's a stereotype and a misconception. I don't think that promiscuity is characteristic of the gay community any more than it is of the straight community. I know several homosexual couples who have the most committed relationships I have ever seen.
The advent of AIDS makes monogamy more of an issue than ever before. Fortunately, lesbians are the group least susceptible to AIDS, but every single person alive should be concerned.
The real issue that society should be concerned with is violent sexuality. It has become more of a social crime to love someone of the same sex than it is to be violent toward someone of the opposite sex. In many circles, homosexuality is condemned more readily than rape.

Looking back, would you choose to do anything differently?

I am glad I have had the courage to follow my dreams and my truth. It has been a more difficult road than the one I was previously on, but I am a much stronger and more loving person because of it.

The Vision Quest

Gina was faithfully married to John for over twenty years even though he didn't have time for her. Having always put her family first, she finally began to pay attention to her own needs. She fell in love with a man who was redesigning her house, and the inevitable triangle evolved: Peter didn't want to lose his job, John didn't want to lose his wife, and Gina didn't want to lose her lover.

Gina

Why did you marry your husband?

As a little girl, my parents were divorced. Actually, my mother had been married twice, divorced twice, and then widowed twice. I lived with her during her first two marriages and suffered severe physical abuse from both of my stepfathers. My real father left us when I was five. Although I felt loved by him, I also felt abandoned and neglected after he left our family. He told me over the phone that he couldn't come to visit because it would tear him up inside.

Ironically, my mother divorced my father because she was having an affair. She divorced him in Mexico, and the next day she married her lover. When I married, I desperately wanted to marry into a real family. It was important to me to have that security, one of the reasons why I chose John. There had been no divorce in his family, which seemed stable and secure.

Not knowing what it meant to be in a conventional family, I conformed to the rules, even though I didn't like what I was doing. I decided that what I felt wasn't important. I was expected to maintain an image that would elevate my husband in society's eyes. I concentrated on what was good for him, always building him up, always maintaining the family image in the community. Appearance was everything. I had to say the right things, dress the right way, go to the right parties, and socialize with the right people. Every aspect of my life was out of my hands, even down to where we went on vacations and what kind of car I drove.

I can't say it was all my husband's fault—it was also his parents'. They gave us our home, so we were expected to throw huge parties for the charities they supported, always command performances. All of a sudden, I would get an invitation in the mail inviting me to a party at my own house. No one ever asked me if it was okay, no one would even call ahead of time to clear the date with me. I was expected to be the consummate hostess, like it or not. Once we were even asked for a donation to one of these parties. I felt violated, a prisoner in my own home.

When did things begin to change?
Something deep inside began telling me that I wasn't happy in my marriage. After we had been married about ten years, I remember saying to myself, "I will give this situation just so long, and if things don't change, *I* will make the changes." But I did nothing.

About five years ago, my in-laws held one of their big parties at our house, but this time we were going to be out of town. I hired a couple to stay at the house and watch our kids for the weekend. Because it was the middle of summer, the party was to be held outdoors, and by agreement, no one was supposed to come inside. Even though my in-laws promised that this rule would be observed, I returned home to total chaos. People had been all over the house, in my bedroom and in my closet—they had even looked through my drawers. The smell of cigarette smoke was everywhere. The baby-sitters remarked, "This is outrageous. How can you stand this?" Then I realized just how angry I was.

I finally told his family that I resented their bribing the kids with a $50 bill to leave the party. I added, "You have been pushing me around for years, but I won't let you do it to my children." But John saw nothing wrong. He felt that we shouldn't complain because we owed his parents for everything they had done for us over the years. He was interested only in what his parents thought.

Did alcohol play a role in the demise of your marriage?
A major role. John would barely be in the door with the bag of groceries before the ice was clinking in his glass. He would have two doubles of some hard liquor before he even began to make dinner. He drank so he didn't have to feel.

When I drank with him, we would talk, but we seemed to progress into an argument pretty quickly, so I stopped drinking with him. If I didn't agree with everything he said, he would insult me by saying I didn't know anything, and he would accuse me of making things up. When I would state how I felt in simple terms, he would start to ridicule the validity of my feelings.

We would usually share some wine with dinner, and I would start cleaning up before he had even finished eating because I couldn't sit there any longer. I used to love him, but I found I couldn't love him anymore. He seemed so ugly, I wanted to get away from him as fast as I could and lock myself in my bedroom.

It was a cold war, a deadly silence. Every time I tried to open up and share something with him, he would ridicule me. So, I just stopped opening up.

What did you do then?

Soon after, I started going to counseling and was told that I was co-dependent. I didn't know what co-dependency meant, so I began to read books. I realized that while I was willing to protect my children, I had been neglecting my own inner child. I kept a picture of myself as a child near my bed. When I began to feel bad, I would look at the picture of little Gina and ask myself, "How can I let people treat you this way?" I began to protect myself from the abuse I had been tolerating for years, and I began to wake up.

At first, I thought John would be supportive, that this could be an adventure for us both, something we could go through together. But he denied that he had ever experienced any kind of abuse, although I knew that his parents had abused him by subtle manipulation and material bribery. Then all hell broke loose in my marriage. He got angry and accused me of stirring things up. He tried to make me think I was crazy, and he destroyed any self-help books I brought into the house. When I started taking control of my life and got stronger, he knew that he couldn't dominate me anymore, and he felt threatened.

I learned about establishing boundaries, how to tell the difference between myself and another person, that I wasn't obliged to take on John's problems. They had nothing to do with me; they had to do with him. When I learned how to exist within these boundaries, John couldn't manipulate me. That made him really mad.

What was day-to-day life like with your husband?

There were so many control issues. I would be at home all day, and John would insist on bringing home the groceries. He didn't want me to drive to town and waste money on gas. He said he wanted to make it easier for me by saving me the trip, so he would bring home the food and make the dinner, which took away that part of my domain.

When we started remodeling the house, we chose a southwest Indian-style theme. So, I began studying Native American culture, mythology, and philosophy. At first, the whole family was into it, and I brought certain elements of ceremony and ritual into our home, like burning sage for purification. At first they loved it, but when I decided to do a vision quest in the desert, they really thought I had flipped out. I did that was to mark a passage from childhood into adulthood, to become responsible for making my own choices, but there was something deeper. I wanted some clarity about my marriage, so I went away and sat out in the desert alone for three nights and three days.

Did you ever try to go to counseling with John?

He refused. He did go for a while but after I found him with another woman, he refused to go back.

Did you ever confront him about his affairs?

The first time I found out about one of his affairs was the day before I learned I was pregnant with my first child. A couple of friends were visiting; the man flew home and left his fiancée who was driving north on a vacation. During the night, I woke up and realized my husband wasn't in bed with me. I didn't know where he was. When I got a flashlight and shone it into the guest room, I saw two bodies move apart. It was shattering, especially since they both knew I was going for a pregnancy test that day.

Every time I confronted John about this kind of thing, he denied it, even when the evidence was damning. Then I found out about a long-term affair he had with a neighbor we had been friends with for years. When I found out, I asked her husband about it; he admitted that he knew all about it, but when he confronted John, John denied it. For years, everyone had known but me. Finally I asked her myself, and she said that she loved him and wanted to be with him. By this time she was separated, maybe even divorced from her husband. John *still* denied it, until I caught them together in our hot tub. It's a profound impact when you actually *see* your partner being intimate with someone else; I think it's worse than just hearing about it. And those are only the times I know about.

Have you ever had an affair?

Yes. But only after twenty years of being faithful.

Is it easy or hard to talk about?

It's easy, yet it's painful to feel so deeply. The more capable I am of feeling pain, the more capable I am of feeling love.

Can you describe how it happened?

When we decided to remodel our house, John hired a friend, Peter, to be our contractor. He had worked for us for about four years. He was charming and good-looking. He was always friendly and had beautiful, clear eyes, and he wasn't afraid to make eye contact. When I looked into his eyes, I felt like I was looking into a mirror. He was a reflection of something inside me that I hadn't experienced before.

The affair began on an emotional level, way before it ever existed on a physical level. While John was a workaholic, Peter would pay attention to my children. John would proudly refer to himself as the absentee father. He was out there making money, and that was what a man was supposed to do, but the children were suffering, and I was suffering. He didn't have time for us. Here was this other man who was gentle, who had time to do things with us. He could talk to me and the children on a deep, inner level. He also saw that I was not being treated properly by my husband. And so we became friends.

After four years of this, one time we kissed, and then all of a sudden it changed. We opened Pandora's Box.

Do you think that having an affair is immoral?
No, but if you're totally committed to someone, there should be no need to have an affair. Trust is the most important thing in a relationship. If the trust is broken between two people, it can be very hard to heal.

Would you consider yourself monogamous?
Yes.

What do you think of other people who have affairs?
It depends. A married woman admits to her husband that she is attracted to another man because she needs some attention. He says, "I don't have time for you. Why don't you find yourself a lover?" Tell me, what is she supposed to do? I don't think it's immoral to have an affair if your needs aren't being met. The better way to handle it, of course, is to get out of a bad marriage first before falling in love with someone else, but life doesn't always work out that way.

Before I had an affair, I always thought there was something fascinating about other people who did. Officially, I thought it was morally wrong, but in the back of my mind there was always something exciting about it, like reading a dirty novel. However, if I heard that someone I knew was having an affair, I would be judgmental. Now I see that people are taking care of their needs, and I don't judge them anymore. I think that people do change and can outgrow each other. I also believe it's possible to love more than one person at the same time. I don't approve of people who have affairs just for the sex, but if it's an affair of the heart, then love rules. We all deserve to be loved.

Did the affair affect your life positively?
In the beginning, it affected my life in a very positive way. It opened up my heart. I felt beautiful all the time. Everything excited me. I became creative; I wanted to paint; I wanted to garden. The birds sang and I heard them. I became alive, sensually alive, physically alive, so alive that I didn't want to lose that feeling. I recognized later that what I was feeling was really coming from me. It wasn't Peter who was giving it to me. I projected that energy onto him and it was reflected back to me.

It also inspired me to move a lot of energy that was blocked inside. It made me realize that I didn't want to live in a situation where I couldn't be who I really was. I needed to feel loved. You can't feel loved by someone who ignores you. When I was with John, I was invisible. He didn't *see* me. I felt as if I were locked up in a cage, and I had to ask myself how I could allow it. My most important goal was to be free of that cage.

How did you get free of that cage?

Peter and I had such a beautiful time. When sexual energy gets going, you can't really stop it. There's this beautiful flower and the bee comes along and just has to pollinate it. It's just natural; you can't stop that energy. It was very disappointing for me because Peter really wasn't available; he already had a family and he was committed to staying with them. I didn't really understand why we had crossed over that boundary between friendship and romance if he wasn't going to make some fundamental change in his life.

From the beginning, I knew it was wrong to go into a love affair that would break up families, but then, it seemed so natural, it was easy to imagine creating a new family with him. I was surprised when it didn't progress in that direction. Peter said he didn't love me in the same way I loved him—he called his feeling for me lust. I tried to understand what that meant. It made me question what happened to the friendship once lust entered into the picture. Just because the friendship went to another level, to me it was enhanced, more powerful, but it wasn't that way for him. I had to accept that he wasn't willing to hurt other people.

Did your husband find out about Peter?

Yes.

Was he willing to call it even, considering you both had affairs?

No. Somehow it was okay for him to have affairs, but not me. In his mind, there are different rules for a woman than there are for a man.

Do you hold Peter responsible for breaking up your marriage?

Looking back, I don't think it was the affair that broke up my marriage. Deep down inside, I knew for years that things weren't right. Peter just ended up playing a part in the drama. It was inevitable; my marriage was coming to an end anyway, not because of Peter, but because of me—I wanted more in life. Now I see that it really wasn't love I was feeling for either of the two men. It was the love I found for myself.

How did John find out about the affair?

He asked me and I told him. I had denied myself for so long that I wasn't thinking about anybody other than me. Ordinarily, I would never betray a friend's confidence, but I was feeling at such a deep level, I just wanted to tell the world. I was tired of denying who I was. I wanted to share my life with Peter.

I decided that I didn't want to hide my feelings. I wanted only to honor what was true for me. So, I didn't lie. That is the biggest thing that I have learned: truth, no matter what the price.

What happened when John found out about the affair?

He got angry and felt violated by the whole situation. He felt he didn't know who I was anymore. I admitted that I cared about Peter, that he was a special person to me. We had a fight, and I went to sleep at a friend's house. Later on, I found out that John had become violent with Peter, and that Peter refused to press charges against him.

How did the affair affect your life negatively?

It broke my heart. I was deeply in love with Peter. I don't think I had ever experienced love on that level before, but it had nowhere to grow. That was the hardest part. It was probably the most painful loss of my life. I am sad that what was beautiful in the beginning, the friendship, had to die.

What price have you paid for your freedom?

I don't really feel as if I had to pay a price. I feel such relief that I have sovereignty over my own life, saying yes to myself, after denying myself for so many years. I am not pining away the way I was before—I am not a prisoner anymore.

You had what most people spend their life trying to achieve, yet you were willing to walk away from it. Do you see letting go of all these material things as a sacrifice?

I don't feel that I have lost anything. I really loved the place where we lived, but I am going to love my life wherever I live. Each situation has its own gift. Things don't make me happy, they're just things. I could live in the Taj Mahal, but if I were locked up inside, how could I enjoy it?

What are your feelings for your husband and your lover now that it's all in the past?

I want what's best for both of them, to be able to feel their feelings and to go on. I myself want to start a new life, I want to be sent away with their blessings, and I want to do the same for them. My path with them is forgiveness—each of them. In order to go forward in my life, I have to forgive, forget, and let go. And they need to forgive me too, or it will hold us back. I recognize that we are all here to learn lessons from each other. Even though we're finished, we'll always be connected. On some level, we are all one. I've read that cliché in a lot of books, but now I know what it means.

I still feel love in my heart for them, but not on a romantic level, where I want to share the deepest part of my soul.

Is there another woman in your husband's life?
Yes.

Do you resent that?

It doesn't bother me in the least, because I think she's done a lot for him. She's inspired him to take better care of himself. He's not drinking so heavily anymore. He's spending more time as a father. Maybe that's what it took. Maybe she was able to awaken something in him that I couldn't. I was shut down; I couldn't talk to him. Maybe he needs a new life too. You know, we all get stale sometimes.

What have you lost as a result of this experience?

Losing material things is not going to matter. I had everything, but I had nothing at the same time. Fortunately, I didn't lose my children; we have joint custody. However, I did lose my innocence and trust, and that does matter.

How did your having an affair, like your mother, affect your relationship with her?

I no longer judge her the way I did as a child after she was divorced from her second husband and was looking for her third. I used to resent her terribly; I thought she was a whore. Now it has come full circle, since I realize that this is probably how my son sees me. I hope in time that my son can forgive me as I have forgiven my mother. During all of this, she has been a gem. She has cried all my tears with me—she really understands.

Is having an affair something you would do again?

I hate to think so. Now that I am free, I can do whatever I want. But I don't think I am the kind of person who wants to have lots of lovers. And I feel such a need to be honest that I don't think I would ever betray another person again.

What if you fell in love with someone who is married?

I would just say no. It has been a hard lesson, and I don't want to go through that again.

Do you want to be in a monogamous relationship again?

Sexually, I want to be monogamous. I can't see myself having more than one partner. It goes against the grain of who I am. To be sexual with someone means opening up and sharing my soul. I'm very selective about whom I want to share that deepest part of myself with. It's sacred.

I want to share a commitment with someone who is as capable of loving me as I am of loving him. I desperately want a relationship with someone, but I want my freedom too. I want us to be able to come and go as we please. I want to be with someone who is committed to me on a spiritual level, who isn't trying to control me and doesn't lie to me. I want mutual respect. I want equality, appreciation, and trust.

What vision have you gained from this experience?

I have gained a sense of wholeness. I used to feel so disconnected from myself, dismembered. My whole body felt as if it were chopped up. All my energies were fragmented, and nothing felt whole. Then I realized that I was disconnected from the source of power within myself as an intuitive, wise woman who knows all the answers. The little girl inside me who was actually running the show needed the guidance of the wise woman.

When I came back from the desert, I had a dream—I was sitting on some rocks high up on a mountain ledge, and I heard footsteps behind me. I turned around and saw this beautiful, slender woman with light shining from her eyes. I knew I should embrace her. When I touched her and held her in my arms, I cried and said, "But you are me."

Now I see that all I have really been afraid of is myself.

The Other Woman

Having recently ended her own long-term marriage, Diana was ready for a real commitment and found Evan who was unfortunately committed to someone else. Unable to decide between two women, each representing a different side of himself, Evan's confusion left Diana high and dry.

Diana

How did you get involved in an affair?

Evan and I were friends. We would find all kinds of things to do with each other: we ran together, we took walks—all without being sexually intimate. When we finally acknowledged the intimacy and lust that was so obvious between us, we referred to it as Pandora's Box. We realized that to open that box would bring a world of troubles and probably destroy our friendship, so we had to keep that lust in the box with a string wrapped around it. But I could feel that string being tugged on every time we touched, and little by little it came undone.

Because he was living with Annie, we weren't supposed to be physical together because he would have to lie to her. He wasn't able admit to her what was going on and didn't tell her about the time we spent together. So rather than lie, we just denied it and kept it secret for a long time—it must have been about five months. During this whole time we were in constant communication with each other. We talked on the phone every day, maybe every other day, and we saw each other every few days. Even though we both have incredibly busy schedules, we would find the time to spend at least a few hours together.

Did you have any idea what you were getting yourself into?

Even from the beginning, I questioned our chance encounters. From the moment he walked into my life, I knew he was everything I had ever dreamed of. Yet how could this be, since he was living with someone else?

Once, when Annie was away he invited me to come up to his house. It was very early in our friendship. Then he called to say that she had come home early, but that I could come up anyway. I said no, that I didn't think I should. It was obvious to me that we had been denying the true nature of our relationship right from the start. Later on I asked him to come down to my house. When he said he couldn't, I got very upset and wrote him a long letter. I said that even though we hadn't kissed, this was more than a friendship and we both knew it. I told him that if his relationship with her wasn't a forever thing, he should get out of it and come to me a free man.

What did he tell you about his relationship with Annie?
He said that he had discussed having children with her, but now he knew that the relationship wasn't really working. He didn't have very good communication with her; he and I talked about all kinds of things—books, philosophy, things like that. He wasn't on the same wavelength with her, which left a big hole in his life. Finally, he told me that he didn't want to continue his relationship with her.

Did you know that you were being set up as the other woman?
I truly believed that it would be over between them some time, but Annie was so dependent on him, emotionally and financially, that it was very hard for him to break it off. I have had several dependent relationships myself, so I know how that is. For a long time I trusted his integrity and thought that he would find a way to end it with her.

We did, at a certain point, cross the line of intimacy. I believed he did not tell her about me in order to end the relationship gracefully without hurting her.

How did you feel about the secrecy?
Fortunately, I didn't have to lie to anyone. Most of the time we spent out of doors. Maybe that was the greatest appeal to me, to spend time being intimate with him in nature. I am very much of an outdoor person. That is where my soul is, like Artemis, the Greek goddess who ruled the wilderness. I am not the type to be contained in a house. I like my house, but I am more in my element when I am down by the cliffs overlooking the ocean, on some windswept ridge of mountains, or by a waterfall. But I missed the fact that I couldn't occasionally get dressed and be taken out. We never did the things couples normally do, like going out dancing and spending the night together. The one time we did go out for dinner, choosing a restaurant was a bit of problem. We couldn't find one where there wouldn't be anyone who knew us. Try *that* in a small town.

Did Annie eventually find out about you?
Yes. It became very obvious to everybody what was going on between us. People told her, and she came and confronted me. I felt very sorry for her because I knew how betrayed she must have felt. She told me he had told her that there was no commitment, that they had to take things one day at a time. But his lying to her and keeping our affair a secret infuriated me. I couldn't stand it. I had to stand there and talk to her, keeping quiet about things that had gone on between us in order to defend him. It was hard to honor my love

for him, and yet be an honest person at the same time. I just couldn't do it. It had been tormenting me for a long time. To sit there and try to deal with her was more than I could handle, yet I felt so sorry for her that she had been betrayed and lied to.

I just kept looking at her. She was yelling at me and calling me all kinds of terrible things: a backstabber, the other woman. But she looked so haggard and tired. I just wanted to take a brush and brush her hair and say, "Don't go home to him looking like that."

I couldn't stand how she looked and felt. I couldn't stand how *I* looked and felt. So I called to tell him that Annie had been there. He said that he would call me and I said, "No, don't." I've seen very little of him since then. He did stay with her. They got married and had a baby. But in the meantime, we have talked. He told me that he didn't have the courage to have a relationship with a woman like me, that it's much easier to be in a relationship with a woman who is dependent on him. He knew that she would always be there for him.

Do you still feel connected to him?

I had a strange dream after a long time had gone by—it seemed like an eternity but was probably only been a few months. In my dream, I saw some silver threads leaving my body: one from my head, one from my heart, and one from my abdomen. I thought they were very interesting, so I decided to follow them. As I followed them, they got thicker and thicker, until I was standing in front of him. And these silver beams were now big shafts of light connecting us at the head, the heart, and the solar plexus. In my dream, I reached out my hands to his and he to mine. As our hands met, there was something cold in our hands—cold and hard and metallic. He asked, "What is that?" And I said, "It's a sword." He asked, "What's it for?" And I answered, "To cut us apart. And you have to do it, because I don't want to." He said, "I don't have the courage." And that was the end of the dream.

In real time, I called him and we got together. I asked him to do what happened in my dream. I held out my two hands and said, "In one hand, I have the chalice of love, and in the other hand, I have the sword to cut us apart. Take one or the other." And he couldn't do either.

And so, our connection lasted well beyond the time of our friendship and the time of our intimacy. For two years, things would happen. I woke up one morning from a really strange dream, which wasn't at all about him, but my first thought upon waking up was: "I wonder if he dreamed about me last night?" I hadn't spoken to him for several months. When I got home that afternoon, there was a call on my answering machine saying, "I dreamed about you last night."

In your mind, is the other-woman scenario an impossible one?

Looking back on my conversations with him, he was looking for a way to make it work. He wanted to have this sweet and wonderful homemaker and his friendship with me, too. For some, this duality is not impossible. I am sure there are people who can accept a limited relationship in their home life and have something else outside their marriage, but I really want the whole thing. I deserve it, so I walked. Despite how painful it was, I felt as if I had to break my heart to save my soul.

Do you have any anger?

Strangely enough, no. I know that it's inappropriate to call and congratulate him on their new family. I do wish them well though. It's going to be a tough marriage. There will be a time of bliss with the children. But I think there are things that he needs that he's never going to find in his marriage, that he will always be looking in other places. The drama that was set up between the three of us will be repeated, but not with me. She's terribly, terribly defensive and jealous. She's the typical Hera archetype and he's the typical Zeus—in love with all women. They keep playing out this scenario, and probably have for so many lifetimes it's ridiculous.

In a lot of ways, he was my equal, my twin, and that's what I'm looking for, but I don't want it to be sneaky. I want someone who can be there for me all the time, someone to call my best friend and lover. I never want to call my lover again and hear, "I can't be with you tonight because she's here." Excuse me, but I think more of myself than that. I deserve more.

My anger's not toward him but more toward life. Sometimes I am angry because that's the only time in my life I have ever felt so intensely in love and so connected to someone. It makes me wonder, does this love exist because I can't have him? Is the intensity there only *because* I can't have him? And the part of me that is really angry says, "Is that it? Is that all I get in this lifetime? Of really loving someone? Is that it?"*That* is what I am outraged about. What can you do though? I guess the saving grace is that I still have me. Had I stayed in my marriage or in the situation of being the other woman, it would have killed me. It would have destroyed who I am. I still have me, but I hate the loneliness.

I have spent most of my life alone. I grew up alone; I was the last child born very late to my mother, who immediately launched her career. My father was always off traveling, and when he was home, he drank heavily. I never really did have parents. My sister and brother are a great deal older than I am. I grew up way out in the country and I spent my entire childhood alone. To have that incredible, intimate connection with a man was something totally new to me.

Aloneness is okay, but I can't quite handle the loneliness. There's a loneliness now that never leaves me, that nags and propels me. It has taken two and a half years to be open enough to try and love somebody else, but I don't know if I will ever be able to do it and have them love me back. I don't know if that will ever happen again.

It goes even deeper. If you've grown up without any real connection with your parents, without any real love, it's hard to create a love affair that lasts. At some fundamental level, there must be a part of me that still believes I don't deserve it, because if I deserved it, I would have had it from day one. It's ironic, because I am a very partner-oriented person, relationships are what I am about. And I do *not* want to spend the rest of my life alone. I have very close men friends whom I share wonderful experiences with, and I have very close, long-lasting relationships with my women friends, but not to have that with one intimate partner has left a hunger in me, a hunger I didn't know before. I am lonely now.

Did you ever have an affair before?

Yes, and that too was insane. I had been married for nine years and was terribly unhappy, but it was crazy for me to get involved with this person. He didn't even like children, and I had children. He was a recluse, and I am fairly social. It was nuts, totally nuts.

Why did you let it happen?

I just needed someone to appreciate me. My husband had completely negated who I was. His way of controlling me was to put me down—for ten years. I was feeling so old, so ugly, so dead inside, and this new man made me feel alive again. But the only way I could cope with having two men—and it didn't go on for very long—was to get my husband out of my house. I must have been crazy. My husband is a good man who has a really good heart. When I look back at it, I see that I was insane, totally insane to let go of him, but it was the only way I could deal with the guilt. I could not possibly be with this other man and go home to my husband. After my husband left, I spent the next two years trying to get this other man out of my life. He was totally dependent on me financially and physically. Afterward I went right into the opposite triangle of being the other woman.

So, you made the ultimate sacrifice of giving up the security of your marriage to tell the truth and honor who you are.

Yes, *then* I gave up the one love of my life.

In what way was your affair a gift to you?

Life puts us here to learn, and I learned a great deal about myself. There's nothing like having an affair to make you question your own integrity, your own honesty. It makes you pull yourself apart and put yourself back together. You have to look at all the aspects of life and love; you have to figure out what you need and what you don't need. You have to look right down to the core of *who you are*. That's what it was for me. That's what Pandora's Box is. You open the box and look inside, and guess what it is? You! You're inside and you have to look at yourself!

The soul-searching probably began long before I was the other woman. However, it continues, and now it's a lifelong process. I could go on and on about being neglected and abused, from a dysfunctional family and all that crap, but it's way beyond that now. I am who I am, because that's who I was born to be. My parents played their role in the drama. At times, when I look at the whole thing, it's this big cosmic riddle. When the insights come, I really get some good laughs out of it. As much as I cry, I laugh. And then there are times when I'm on more of an even keel, when I'm not laughing and I'm not crying. It just is what it is, and I just dance with it.

Do you feel as though you have learned to dance with your demons?

I was a great dragon slayer for years. The demons kept popping up and I would slay yet another one. I would get so tired and would just want to rest for a minute, then there would be another one. Demons, demons, demons—there were so many. I wanted to put on my business card: Entrepreneur and Dragon Slayer Extraordinaire. You have dragons? I will come slay them for you—hah—me and my mighty sword. But I feel that ceasing the dragon slaying is ending the masculine part of my life. It's a very masculine thing to do to go out and wave a sword around. I'm really ready to slide quite happily into being a woman. I want to enjoy that part of my life. It's strange now when I feel myself dealing from my masculine side, because I've dealt from that side for so long. My affair was a big part of discovering who I am, discovering my more feminine side. I am tired of dragons. They pop up and I say, "Oh, silly dragon, would you like some chocolate chip cookies?" I am really tired of slaying them. I'd rather feed them.

It's the same with my sexuality. I really love the physical part of my life. Instead of seeing it as this dragon, I see it as a wonderful gift. I would like to feed it—just let it be this bubbly dragon, snorting fire, causing little fires here and there. Fires are beautiful, but most people see them and just want to put them out. I am tired of putting out fires. I like the fires—I want to let them burn and brighten the darkness.

In looking back on your experience, why do you think people have affairs? Why does it happen?

Lord, I don't know. I was totally unprepared for the whole thing. I had heard of my friends having affairs and I had seen their pain, but I was totally unprepared for what it really felt like. It has made me very aware. Now when I know someone who is involved in an affair, or on the verge of getting involved, I completely understand what that person is about to go through or has been through and I can empathize. My advice is: "Don't bother. Don't bother until you are ready to go through the fire. And if you play with fire, play to win."

Some people do win. Some people have an affair and end up with that man or woman they fell in love with, but they pay an awful, awful price. People do what they are going to do, no matter what you tell them of your own experience. I am not about to deny anyone's experience or judge them for it, but I think there are people we are cosmically drawn to, and the lessons we are here to teach each other are nothing like the ones we *thought* we were going to learn. And the adventures we are given are not of our making. As John Lennon said, "Life is what happens when you've made other plans."

If you had it to do over again, would you do it any differently?
Do you mean would I open the box? I don't know. Yes, probably. What would I do differently? I guess I would fight for the man I love. I would have accepted the duality of the situation. I would have phoned her and said, "I am really sorry that you feel this way. I am sorry that you have been hurt, and I am sorry that he hasn't been honest with you, but I really love him, and I have a right to be in his life. I am not leaving." That's what I would have done differently. I was the one who left, and I left them together. I didn't say, "Come back later," or anything like that. I just split. If you fold, you lose. You're out of the game. She's his. I don't know what's ahead for them, but I think I should have just stood my ground and said, "I'll leave when he asks me to. I have a right to be in his life." And I would have challenged him, too.

Do you know how he feels?
I hear he misses me.

Does love triumph in the end?
Only the love of yourself. To thine own self be true. I don't know about all the rest of it. I'm still hoping that true love exists. There seems to be two types of men: the ones who are hooked on dependent women, and the ones who are hooked on independent women. Hopefully, there's a man who appreciates me for who I am, yet can stand in his own light.

I am beyond babies and housekeeping. I want to be with someone who will support our mutual growth as individuals and as a couple. I'm strong, but I need to be loved as a woman. I'm human, and I'm strong enough to admit it.

Does love triumph in the end? Ask me when I'm ninety.

Burning Bridges

*Vanessa left an eighteen-year marriage to be with the man of her dreams.
To be with him, she was willing to give up absolutely everything—family,
security, social prestige. In a tragic accident, she lost all she had sacrificed
to attain. Years later, Vanessa has the chance to reflect on the events of her
life and decide, if she had it to do over again, whether she would choose
differently.*

Vanessa

Why do you think people risk everything to have an affair?

Due to my Victorian upbringing, my thinking on this has gone from an
extremely conservative point of view to facing the reality of modern life. I was
taught that one simply did not have affairs. My mother never even discussed
the facts of life with me. I learned about the reality of sex on my own. My
husband, who was ten years older than I, had a lot of experience, and I didn't.
My first sexual encounter was quite a jolt.

*When did you begin to feel that marriage was not the fairy tale you had
been raised to believe in?*

Our relationship was difficult because of his entangled emotions about
the family business. There were expectations he had been raised with that he
could never get away from. Sex for me was very painful after birthing two
children. He couldn't understand it, but he remained faithful.

People told me that Jim was an alcoholic and that I should watch out. I
took a lot of deep breaths, realizing that I had two beautiful babies and was
married into a fine family. It was a dilemma. After we had been married about
seven or eight years, things definitely weren't working between us. Jim was
away on business more than he was home, leaving me all alone in this big,
beautiful house. I was attractive, outgoing, with many friends. Considering
the circumstances, having an affair was something that was bound to happen.
I wasn't looking for anything in particular; men just liked me.

Meanwhile, things were not going well for Jim, business-wise, and I saw
the torment he was going through. I begged him to quit the family business.
I knew it was killing him; I knew it was killing us. He said, "I can't." I knew
it was the end, but I was determined not to let him down. I was not going the
let the company do him in. I hung in there, but that's when I got involved in
an affair. I was surrounded by temptation and I fell in love with somebody
else.

Did you want to leave your marriage?

No. It was just a comfort to have a warm and loving hug from someone who loved me. There were other men who would drop by during the day to see me, respectable people. A husband can't leave a wife alone like that and not expect something to happen.

Did you feel that what you were doing was okay?

Not really. I was confused and unhappy. This other man was also having a difficult time in his marriage, and we shared something in common, but I had no intention of leaving my marriage, or spending the rest of my life with him.

How did it end?

We moved away. There was a chance for Jim to start over in the same company but in a different place. So we went.

Did anyone ever confront you about this affair?

A few family members knew about it. Once I had too much to drink at a party and my mother-in-law confronted me about my behavior. She was right—I had not conducted myself as a lady.

Did your husband know what was going on?

At that particular party, he wasn't even aware of it. It wasn't until we went to a series of farewell parties just before we moved away that Jim had it out with my lover. Apparently, by that time he knew. It was very unpleasant. But he never talked to me about what happened. He was in complete denial about it. All he said was, "Go have an affair if you need to, but just stay married to me." I felt he was completely missing the point. That's not who I am. I wanted to be with only one man and he gave me his permission to do whatever I pleased. That was the worst thing he could have said. To me, it was an indication that he didn't care.

Were you relieved to move away?

Yes, I wanted us to have another chance. The marriage should have ended then. Everyone knew it, but I can see that only after the fact.

There are two sides to the story though. I had two very ill parents who took a lot of my time. Out of loyalty to them, I wasn't always there for Jim either.

Did you miss your lover?

Oh, yes. Even after we moved away, I had to go back to take care of my parents so the affair continued. There was still a tremendous amount of love and affection there.

What happened after you moved away?

I didn't seek out any new relationships, but after I joined a tennis club, I began to meet new people. I made social connections that helped Jim's business, but things in our marriage did not improve. One Christmas I felt so depressed that I attempted suicide. I may have done it to find out if he really loved me. After I'd taken all the pills, I changed my mind, realizing I didn't want to die. Jim was downstairs, completely unaware of what was going on so I told him to call the doctor. They rushed me to the hospital and I almost died. Afterwards, he sent me flowers, but he still wouldn't talk about what the problem between us was. Nobody would talk about it.

My lover was still trying to see me, but I told him that it was over. However, in many ways I felt he was the only one who really cared about me.

Why did you deny him?

Because my value system told me it wasn't right.

Do you still think it's immoral to have an affair?

No. Not today, but then I did. I decided that it was over and burned all his letters. Determined to make a new life for myself, I decided it was never going to happen again.

When did you finally give up on your marriage?

Jim collapsed and almost died. After he recovered, the company sent him around the world again on business. I was more alone than ever, the same situation as years before all over again, the exact same scenario.

Had you seen a marriage counselor at any time?

Yes. He told me my husband was an alcoholic and I had better get some therapy so I went to therapy alone.

All Jim wanted was sex, but there was no way I could give that to him anymore. I was disgusted. By that time, he was having affairs with other women, especially with a governess who was living in our house. I wasn't even aware of it, until I walked in on them one night.

Did you talk to him about this?

Yes, I told him that we were being taken for a ride, that she was taking over our children, our household, our lives. He said, "Okay, let her go." I fired her the next day.

I found out that he was also having an affair with someone at work. He kept trying to send me on vacations so that I could "relax," and then when I was out of town, he would continue his affairs. After a while, I figured out what was going on. I was angry and confronted him, but he would deny everything.

When did things finally blow up?

He decided to send me away to the Caribbean, but I didn't want to go. One night we went out for dinner at a French restaurant, and afterwards he took me to a travel agency and picked up some plane tickets that were already paid for. Later that night I found him drunk and passed out. I decided that there was no way I could leave, so I went to the phone and canceled the reservations. When he woke up he was very angry and yelled, "You're going whether you like it or not." I was scared, so I threw my things in a suitcase and called a taxi. I almost lost my arm when he slammed the door behind me. I flew stand-by in a state of trauma.

Why did he want you to go so badly?

He said it would be good for me. Ironically, it was on that trip I met the man I would later leave him for. It was the last thing in the world I was looking for, another man. All I wanted was two meals a day, a lot of rest, and a walk on the beach. I minded my own business for the first four days, enjoying my freedom and my health. After a week, I felt better and I was coming out of my shell. I went to a social get-together and that's when I met Ivan. At the end of three weeks, I was supposed to meet my husband at a college reunion in New York, but I knew that I couldn't play the game anymore, and I sent Jim a telegram telling him that I wasn't coming.

I still had no idea I was in love with Ivan, but I did know that there was an attraction between us. Some of the other women could tell that Ivan and I liked each other, and they fixed me up with some new clothes so that I looked really good. One Sunday we had a wonderful day together on an excursion with several other people, but when we got back for dinner, Jim was there.

He was drunk and demanded to know what was going on. I said simply, "What a surprise to see you." We tried to go to a cocktail party and dinner. Ivan was very polite, and Jim was very insulting. My friends told me to leave. There was a confrontation in which Jim accused Ivan of having an affair with me. Jim got violent, went back to my room, and destroyed everything in sight. He tried to set the room on fire and threw half my clothes in the ocean. I was scared to death and spent the night hiding out in my friend's room. I had no idea what was going to happen next—I knew it was over between Jim and me. Ivan was enraged over what had happened and was very protective, not wanting to see me hurt. I wanted to go home to see my children, so he put me on the next plane, tears streaming down my face. He told me he loved me and would be in touch. When I got back home and found that our house was also trashed and that Jim was missing, I decided to file for divorce.

When did you make plans with Ivan about your future together?

When he came to visit me, I told him that I was getting out of my marriage. We realized that we were totally in love, and we agreed to marry. He promised to be by my side.

How did you feel about giving up eighteen years of marriage?

It had to be done before we were all destroyed. Even though Jim begged me to come back, I knew it wouldn't work. I found out I was going to have Ivan's child in the middle of all this, and I was thrilled. He didn't have any children, and I was happy to give him that. I almost died during the pregnancy and almost lost the baby. Ivan was afraid he was going to lose both of us.

How did all this affect your children?

I wanted the best for them and I wanted to let them finish school where they were. So I left them with Jim, and when Ivan and I bought a house on the West Coast, I took only the bare minimum of my possessions with me. I was afraid I was never going to be allowed to see my children again—I was threatened with prison if I ever came back. So I decided to go back and kidnap my kids. I loved my them and knew that I could take care of them.

Did you consider how it would affect your children to be taken from their father?

I felt that Jim was irresponsible, that it wasn't safe to leave them with him. Ivan went with me and he helped me get them.

Looking back on all of this, would you do anything differently?

No. I do regret all the suffering, but as a mother, it was my gut feeling that this was something I had to do. There was no other way I would ever see my children again.

Do you feel that you were judged by people for what you did?

Yes. I felt I was excommunicated from the family, but in the long run, I knew that everyone would emerge healthier and more stable.

Did you feel you had to burn your bridges with the past?

Yes. I finally had an honest, intelligent, alert, and aware person to help me through it all with no words needing to be exchanged. I met my soul mate who brought out the best in me. Our love gave me something I had never experienced before and I felt no remorse.

What was your new life like?

The birth of our son, Sean, was joyous, with my children present, welcoming the baby to our new family. It was a painful delivery, but nothing could be worse than what I had already been through. Ivan really wanted this son. He was high on fatherhood for a long time.

When Sean was five months old, we went to Hawaii on business. Ivan was in the middle of negotiating a deal to manage a new resort, and we were staying in Honolulu—Ivan, the baby, the children, and I. Ivan and my eldest son had a horrendous argument and we put my son on the plane to go home to his father. A couple of days went by and Ivan decided that we should go home, too. I felt that I had ruined his whole trip and I suggested that we spend some time away from the kids before we left. I got a baby-sitter, and we drove to the north side of the island to spend the evening with an old friend of his. I guess we had too much to drink. On the way home, the car spun out of control and crashed. When I woke up in the hospital, he was dead. I was half-dead myself. They had to operate to save my arm.

Why do you think that happened?
Stress and exhaustion. I have a mental blank about everything that happened. I have spent years trying to remember.

How did you feel?
My world came to an end. I couldn't even bear to tell my children what happened.

What has your life been like since then?
I felt as though God spared me for a reason, perhaps to raise Sean. I knew I had to recover so that I could be a mother to all my children. They were all I had left.

Was there ever a reconciliation with Jim in your later years?
Jim remarried, and after Ivan's death, he and his new wife invited me for Thanksgiving. A few years later, we even shared Christmas as a family. And as Sean got older, they invited him to spend time with them during the summer. I feel at peace with Jim now, and I think he feels the same way, although there is still a certain sadness there. I don't think that either of us has the right to be judgmental about what happened. We all suffer at our own levels. The little time I had with Ivan was worth all the years I was married to Jim.

How has your experience affected your outlook on social mores?
Since I went through my marriage and divorce, the times have changed. I think it's good for young people to live together before they make a mess of their lives.

What is your advice to people today who may encounter a similar situation?
To believe in yourself and in a higher power guiding your life that is much bigger than the little "I." Things happen for a reason. Go through what you have to go through. Listen to your heart and look for the truth in a person's eyes. It's good to look at yourself in the mirror, too.

Tolerance is also very important and keeping a broad, open mind to life's possibilities. This is essential at any age. What happened to me could happen to anyone tomorrow.

Have these events taught you your life lessons?
I still think I have a lot of lessons to learn. You've never learned all your lessons. Only God in heaven knows that.

I have learned that I am a valuable person, and that I have the ability to both give and receive. I have learned not to expect too much. Life has taught me to be independent and how to live on my own, but I also feel that I am here for a divine purpose.

Do you feel that there will ever be another man in your life?
I think that Ivan was my one and only true love, but there may possibly be a man who will be a companion in my later years. I am not closing the door on that. I am very open and I'm ready.

How would you feel if you saw your own children going through what you went through?
I would treat them with compassion, understanding, and forgiveness, and I would not take sides. Needless to say, I would be loyal to my own children, but I would also be open to everyone involved.

What do you think it would take for people to go through this life-changing process without so much pain and devastation?
The way our world is today, it takes a rare, strong individual and a dedicated belief in a higher power. If you have that, you can deal with anything. I have never stopped loving my first husband, in spite of all that's happened. Above all, love has to be the guiding force in our lives.

Through the Fire

When Marian found out that her husband, David, had been having an affair with a friend of hers, she was deeply hurt and angry. Dealing with sexual betrayal allowed both people to discover new ways of processing their feelings, and deepening their commitment to each other.

David and Marian

How did the issue of infidelity come up in your lives?
Marian: I don't know if I can talk about this yet. It's not easy . . . it still hasn't completely healed.

Would it be better to ask you these questions in private?
Marian: No, if we have to hide the truth from each other, that's not good either. I don't want to wonder what David's telling you.

Let's begin again. Do you think it's immoral to have an affair?
Marian: No, but I feel that lying or deceit is not acceptable. I've been a sexologist for years studying sexuality in all its forms, and I've had affairs in my first marriage toward the very end when there was nothing left.

What were they like for you?
Marian: They weren't love affairs, but more like anonymous sex—a couple of one-night stands. I was doing it out of defiance, trying to prove my desirability when my marriage was falling apart, the classic divorcée stuff.

Had your first husband betrayed you?
Marian: I don't know. He was an alcoholic who was sexually and emotionally unavailable. I got too lonely and hung on for a very long time until finally I just had to let go.

In a scenario like this do you see having an affair as liberating?
Marian: What happened was perfect. That current of energy had to make itself known, as a wake-up call to life. As a holistic healer, I can't consider any kind of energy wrong. All forms of energy carry us to a state of greater aliveness. I think it's important to own the attractions that we each feel, to bring them up and share them as a couple, not to suppress them. Personally, I do not choose infidelity. I choose to commit myself to an intimate inner circle. To me sex is sacred and is to be experienced within the temple of honesty.

So, you think it's okay for a partner to be attracted, but not okay to act on those attractions?

Marian: Ideally, the attractions are a part of a person's aliveness, but I want to keep the actual physical sex within the boundaries of marriage. It's a challenge for the marriage to expand to embrace the sexual part of a partner's psyche that wants expression. It's a cue to grow, more than a secret diversion that risks the marriage itself.

Does the danger exist in the secrecy—what you call deceit?

Marian: About ninety percent of it. The other ten percent is that I don't want to get a disease like AIDS.

How did you find out about David's affairs?

Marian: By telephone. David was involved with two different women. One had been a student of mine, and the other was in a support group with me. So I knew them both. My former student telephoned Friday morning, terrified because she felt out of control, yet was aware that the affair with David wasn't going anywhere. She knew that I was leaving for the weekend and didn't want him to come to her house while I was away—she was afraid of what would happen. She was so angry she even called the police and accused David of molesting her. After talking to me, she didn't press charges. He was lucky; he narrowly escaped legal actions.

Did she take any responsibility for her role in the situation?

Marian: No. She said she needed the physical ecstasy from the affair, but she didn't take any responsibility for it.

David, can you talk about that relationship?

David: It was amazingly intense. There was tenderness and there was a lot of raw sexuality.

What about the allegations that you molested her?

David: There was mutual consent.

Marian: She said that the affair had originally been consensual, but that six months after the affair ended, David kept coming to her door uninvited. He entered her home against her wishes, initiated sexual behaviors that she resisted, and persisted when she refused. She said he seemed to be in an altered state, and that's when she realized that it wasn't her he was after but the high of an altered state. She did not feel loved, appreciated, or included at all.

The second woman *didn't* come forward. As a matter of fact, she lied when we asked her to stay away. She couldn't understand that we didn't want anything to do with her and proceeded to telephone several more times. It wasn't in my heart to talk to her.

David, what gave you permission to have a relationship outside your marriage?

David: I didn't feel good about it when I was doing it, but I had some needs that weren't being met. I didn't address those needs to Marian in a way that they could be resolved within the framework of our marriage. There were strong forces going on within myself that are labeled by therapists as "love addiction."

Can you describe what those forces are like?

David: It's a need to be acknowledged. I was looking for that acknowledgment outside myself rather than from within. I moved away from my own center and looked for sexual validation through other women. I know now that I can't get it from Marian or anyone else; I need to find that validation from within my own core.

Knowing that you have this tendency, have you deliberately chosen a partner with the integrity to challenge you? How has this forced you to grow out of your pattern of love addiction?

David: It is a pattern that was operant in my first marriage. It's a pattern in my life of looking to women for acknowledgment of my sexual power. It's amazing to me how available that is if you look for it. There are lots of people out there, both men and women, who are more than willing to give that to each other, regardless of their other relationships. There is a permissiveness in our society, especially in the media, which encourages us to be promiscuous.

Would you say that society does not support the sanctity of marriage?

David: Exactly. I feel very fortunate for the support we need from our extended family, for the healing we have received.

Marian: We have joined a group called "Recovering Couples Anonymous," or RCA, where we go every Friday night. It's for couples who want to work on surrendering to a higher power, similar to the twelve-step program of AA. It's deep, intricate, intense, and beautiful.

Does it help you to feel that you are not alone?

David: Tremendously, especially when people express what they are feeling. I've also been attending a weekly group for "Sex and Love Addicts Anonymous," or SLA. I've heard men talk about the issues that are foremost in their lives and seen them learn how to rely on their higher power. I've seen the anguish and grief of men who have found themselves acting out their sexual issues repetitively. It's helped me realize that I don't want to put my loved ones through that kind of anguish anymore. It has helped me to put my stake in the ground and say, "This is where I take a stand."

I've been able to examine my pattern of a stray thought about a woman becoming dominant. And how that thought can lead to fantasy, intrigue, and inappropriate action. Unfortunately, it's a pattern that many men and women share. Having recognized and examined this pattern, I can now make conscious choices long before I act. Before, it was like a snowball rolling downhill, getting bigger and bigger until it was out of control. Now I am aware of what's happening long before I reach the point of riding downhill on an avalanche.

What advice can you offer men who are caught up in that vicious cycle?

David: Find a confidant, counselor, or therapist whom you can trust implicitly, and talk about what's going on. Talk about your unmet needs and look at your history. Explore other ways to meet those needs within your current relationship. If you are involved in a dangerous or harmful relationship, look at who, including yourself, can get hurt and determine if you really want that to happen. If you want to get out of the relationship, get the help you need. See if you're involved in a repetitive pattern. If you need validation, look for ways to get that validation from within yourself, the only place you can really find it. Looking for that validation outside yourself is ultimately an exercise in illusion, frustration, and futility. Also, decide if you want to be in a committed relationship and be honest about it.

Marian: I would like to see intimacy schools conducted by qualified couples' counselors. Many of us have never known what true intimacy is all about—we have no models. As children and as adults, we're not taught about intimacy, sex, and money. We just wing it.

What has the pain of this healing process been like for you? People need to understand that there is a way out.

Marian: When I found out about David's affair, I bottomed out into hopelessness. My immediate response was that I didn't believe we had a future. It broke out into the open one Friday morning, and that very night we got immediate help.

The nightmare for most people is in being discovered, when all the fears come flying out of Pandora's Box. Could you possibly share what that process was like for you, and how you worked through it? How did you get each other back onto solid ground?

Marian: At first, when the woman phoned and told me what had happened, I went into a stage of disbelief, thinking she was trying to get even with me for something else. I asked David to get on the phone with her and address the accusations that he had been sexually molesting her, but when he picked up the phone, she hung up. I knew I wasn't going off for the weekend and asked him to sit down and tell me the truth. When he told me, I ran up and down the stairs yelling, "Get out, get out!" But when I had to decide what to do next, I reached out for help.

David, you must have been terrified. It must have been your worst nightmare coming true.
David: It was. I went into a state of uncontrollable sobbing. I was afraid I was going to lose Marian.

What were your feelings about the other woman?
David: I felt that she was seriously exaggerating: I hadn't molested her. I also perceived that I had been temporarily out of touch with reality, trapped in my own illusion. I had also involved myself with someone who was relatively unstable.

Were you angry at her?
David: I was angry at her for saying I had molested her, for calling the police, and for her not owning up to her part in it.

Did you feel any sense of loss over your relationship with her ending?
David: I was glad it was over. It was a relief.

Marian, where did you go for help?
Marian: I spoke with two friends on the phone, a beloved older woman and my ex-husband. They both gave me love and support which I desperately needed. We went to a group we had heard of, "Recovering Couples Anonymous," which met that very night. Desperate for help, we told the truth right in front of this group of strangers. We had to contain our crisis. When two people have a crisis like this and *don't* reach out, I don't give them much of a chance. They need to be held by a larger, more loving context, usually involving others.
David: The support is absolutely vital. You have to be willing to admit that your life is in total chaos, that it's out of control, and that you need help. It's the first of the twelve steps in any recovery program.

Do you feel that you are through the crisis now?
David: I do.
Marian: I still feel some insecurity. And to this day, we don't reach down into the more primal passionate levels of our sexuality together as we used to. There's something in the way. The trust still needs to heal, but it may go even deeper after this incident. It made us aware that we each have work to do, to dig into the primal dirt.

Do you think that the demonic aspect of an affair comes from maintaining a double life, and withholding the truth from the one you love?

Marian: It creates a split between the heart and the sexual chakra. I've done body work for many years and can feel how armored most people are through the diaphragm. They are literally living in two different worlds: the pelvis wants to go off and live for unbridled raw sex, yet it can't bring the raw sexual energy up into the holier realm of the heart. It's the Madonna-whore complex. The beauty and power of raw sex don't come home.

How can we translate that desire to love in a sexual way into a holy expression—and become whole again?

David: I believe it comes through nurturing ourselves and each other in loving ways.

Marian: I think it has to go deeper than that. It requires going into a primal process within ourselves. The split that happens in relationships is just a reflection of an inner psychic split. It takes the power of a rocket lifting off a launch pad to heal some of that stuff—powerful breath work, Reichian technique, and Gestalt process.

We're just beginning to learn the tools to deal with the solution as well as the problem. It's all about the energy in the first three chakras: the first is survival, the second is sex, and the third is power. My vision is that there will be mass therapy sessions in the future to gather people together in an atmosphere of integrity. Spiritual life is not only about God the Father . . . it's about God the Mother, too—right down here.

You have to do this type of therapy in a climate of strength and safety. When you open Pandora's Box, you don't see black, horrible snakes, but there are wiggly, dark energy patterns that look like snakes which aren't necessarily bad, but have been suppressed for so long that they have to be released and integrated.

When that energy arises, how do you channel it into an appropriate context? How do you take love—the most powerful force in the universe—and transform it into something that isn't going to destroy your life?

Marian: I used to suppress those instincts. Little by little, I am feeling the turn-on, and the turn-on is divine. But there's a difference between letting that turn-on light you up and make you feel alive versus acting it out with gestures and genitals. It's like enjoying the sensuousness of cake and ice cream without gorging on it. The addiction comes through acting out sex unconsciously without any moral intelligence between instinct and action.

David: It also helps to set up alternative choices of behavior. If it's a drink you want, go for a glass of water. If it's sex you want, go for a jog or a bike ride. If you crave sugar, ask for a hug instead. Or just pick up the telephone and call a friend who will support you in resisting the urge. It's the same process with any addiction, whether it's sex or sugar.

Marian: These techniques are temporary devices, but they do teach you to wake up to your patterns.

David: Movement has been really good for me. Although it looks like chaotic dancing to high-energy music, it really helps me blast through my patterns. I get to discharge all that energy: the frustration, rage, and anger at myself, at past relationships, and at Marian. I just get that energy out of the cells of my body so I don't have to hold onto it anymore. I am consciously erasing the cellular memory of past, repetitive experiences that have caused grief, both to me and to my loved ones. Once I discharge that energy, I reprogram it and take time for myself—quiet time for meditation, for walks, for getting centered again.

Do you believe that people with sex addictions are just looking to be loved?

Marian: Yes, and unfortunately even today we are still gender scripted. A lot of that drive to conquest really is the primal drive to wholeness. If girls were raised to climb mountains, and boys were raised to sing softly, we would be able to understand the "gender gap." In the core of our being, we really *are* androgynous.

I feel compassion for the other women in David's life. I see how they were terribly suppressed and needed love, but at the same time I have to respect my own boundaries. Their healing does not need to take place at my expense. I used to have nonexistent boundaries; I was the new-age "queen of love" because I was so forgiving, so it's very good for me to say no.

Do you think that this is something that will ever come up again for you?

David: If I start to feel a strong attraction to someone, I will tell Marian about it and ask her to help me look at what's going on. I would also seek support from others in my network immediately and get the support I need.

Marian: I don't want to stop loving people. It's wonderful to have a precious flow of love among friends, but I do have a tremendous need to enforce my boundaries and say, "You can come only *this* close to me right now."

To what degree are you grateful for the experience that you have had?

Marian: We were and still are in business together. We have been inseparable. Looking back, I see how entangled we were. Something had to give so that each of us could regain a sense of our individual selves.

At that point, I was addicted to my marriage. When my marriage threatened to go belly-up, it forced me to look at my attachment to and dependence on it. Now I feel that we have a healthier balance of time we spend together and time we spend alone. We have joined different groups, and both of us have individual friends. Though I would have preferred to get to this conscious place without such an intense crisis, I guess it was a cosmic wake-up call.

David: I am grateful that we have had this crisis to learn how to support each other. Looking for validation is an issue I have been dealing with for years. Through this, I've discovered places within myself I never knew existed, an inner strength and a healing, inner peace and validation. I've learned how to take time to be with myself by myself, celebrating that divine space within.

Have you found it possible to love other women without making love to them?

David: Yes, I certainly do. I can express the love I feel in my heart for them in appropriate ways. I can be loving and still maintain my personal boundaries.

Would you talk about the element of forgiveness?

Marian: Forgiveness for me is owning my part of it: my own co-dependence, my own addiction to the marriage, and my own abandonment issues from childhood. I'm still healing from the message I got that I don't deserve a man's sustained love and caring. Forgiveness is seeing the lesson in everything that happens.

David: I realized that I didn't feel our home was totally safe for me. My need for an emotionally safe place was not being met. I failed to own it as my home too and define what worked and didn't work for me if we were going to continue the relationship in a mutually supportive way. So I chose to go outside my marriage, instead of choosing to come inside my core and claim its sanctity as a temple.

Marian: I had been erupting in rage attacks, a way of relating what was leftover from my childhood.

David: By coming into the core of my own being and communicating the impact her rage has upon me and the depth of my feelings about her rage, it makes it easier to draw the line between us. Again, it's a matter of understanding our boundaries. I need to be clear about what help she needs and what help I can give, so that there are no more rage attacks.

Marian: He put up healthy boundaries, and I got the message. I slip up once in a while, but it's nothing more than a verbal lashing here and there. Now when the rage comes up, we kneel at our altar together and ask for help.

David: There's something we do called a clearing process that might be helpful to those of you reading this book. When we discover that we are seeing things differently, we sit together and set a timer. I ask Marian, "What is in the way of greater intimacy between us?" She knows she has five minutes of totally uninterrupted time to express herself to me. Maintaining eye contact, we sit cross-legged. We stop standing face-to-face, arms crossed, yelling at each other. There is a humbling that takes place by coming to an altar and kneeling or sitting cross-legged. Lowering ourselves physically changes the whole energy dynamic.

Marian: One of the ground rules is that within those five minutes, I can use only "I" statements. I can't use it as an opportunity to dump on David. At first it takes a lot of attention, but after a while, it's easy.

David: It's a blessing, an oasis in the storm. We do two or three rounds of clearing—or as many rounds as we need. We always end with a round of saying what we appreciate about each other, a vital part of this clearing process. After we have completed the clearing part, it is amazing if we can't immediately find something to say that expresses our appreciation for each other.

Throughout this entire process, we maintain eye contact. And it is so important to breathe together the whole time. There is a harmonic resonance and balancing that takes place through breathing. If you can make it to the appreciations, you will be amazed by what you and your partner can say about each other, things you would not have imagined possible just moments before.

Marian: Alternatively, we will do something called the "ten-minute connection." We just lie down together and breathe in unison for ten minutes. It harmonizes our whole energy field underneath the upset. It brings the sense of "us" back into focus, so that we can handle the two personalities in conflict.

David: We embrace either chest-to-chest or spoon fashion. Usually the person most upset is the one who gets cuddled in the spoon. If it's really volatile, sometimes we'll start with the embrace.

This is really inspiring. Most couples don't have the resources to pull it back together once they've been to the edge.

Marian: Lots of women just accept it as the way men are—that it's okay for them to have affairs. That's what co-dependence is: ignoring the addiction, actually supporting it. If a woman continues to accept her husband's affairs, things will never change for her. In old age, she and her husband will probably just take turns nursing their debilitating illnesses, which I believe are manifestations of their unresolved issues on a subconscious level. The body reflects this kind of suppression, which explains the source of a lot of "dis-ease."

How do you advise women who suppress their rage and jealousy?

Marian: It's very damaging for a woman to spend her life tiptoeing around a man's temper. A woman shouldn't have to live with her boundaries being violated like that. There need to be game rules for fair fighting. She has an equal right to express her anger, but a woman claiming her rage doesn't mean saying that the man is wrong either.

Rage has been much maligned in our culture, especially for women. That's part of the gender gap. Men have permission to have rage, but not tears; whereas women can grieve, but never get angry. It is just the vital red energy of the first chakra coming up. I call it the cork in the bottle of power.

When a woman finds a safe, supportive coach or therapist who can handle it, she can release her rage and let that red energy move. As it moves, it becomes a healthy crimson rather than a bloody red. Women need to feel the power of their rage without dumping it on their partner.

David: One man we knew was physically violent and verbally abusive. Finally, his wife left and didn't let him know where she was living. She would meet with him only if he agreed to go to counseling, a safe place where there were clear game rules. The counselor operated as a referee, and the office was a neutral meeting ground. After several months, he found alternative ways to deal with his stress rather than taking it out on her. They reestablished their trust. Her leaving woke him up to the fact that he was a rage-aholic, and that his life was falling apart. He started owning responsibility for his actions and the grief he has caused in other people's lives.

What is the difference between a man who has affairs and one who is loyal but vents his rage on his wife?

Marian: None really; they're both dysfunctional. It comes down to fear of intimacy.

What do you think of the situation when one person in a relationship wants to grow and the other one doesn't?

Marian: I support the person who is awakening and going for his or her aliveness. Often that person's stand—moving out, asking for mediation or counseling—is a healthy one. There is always hope that the fabric of the relationship can be mended, but often it has to be unknit before it can be reknit. And that unknitting or unraveling is a risk.

But no relationship is worth the price of going back under the covers and not awakening. You can wait until the pain of suppression becomes so great that you erupt. Instead, I recommend using that time when you could consciously be growing. Usually it requires some kind of jolt for the one who refuses to grow. I know that is easier said than done. I hung on to my first marriage way too long. There are times when it's right to let go.

How does a person recognize when it's time to let go?

David: With compassionate and ruthless honesty. My first marriage also lasted far too long.

Marian: Turn to your higher power. Surrender to your own counsel. If one person is willing to grow and the other isn't, then you each have to follow your own path.

Through this whole experience, what have you gained and what have you lost?

David: I have lost a sense of trust without question, a fabric that was woven in Light. Through my betrayals, that fabric has become unraveled. Though there has been a healing process, the loss of trust has been the saddest part. Although I am certain within myself that I now have a commitment to be a lifetime partner with Marian, she no longer is certain. I don't know if we can regain what we had before, but I also sense that this is part of our history together, and now it's a matter of weaving a new fabric.

The blessing is that we have both grown tremendously. We have discovered a deeper relationship with the Beloved within. And we can possibly help heal others.

Marian: It's mostly a blessing. I feel like I woke up from the romantic fairy tale and realized that I really have my husband within myself. That male energy within me has been awakened and growing ever since. I don't have to make David my hero any longer. Sometimes I worry that I will get so strong that I won't even want to be in a marriage. Or maybe I'll just stay in it out of choice rather than need.

There is still some residual victim consciousness within me that feels insecure, but that's healing, too. I believe that David's intentions are sincere in going deeper into matrimony with me, but I still have a certain reserve that if he were to have a secret affair again, I would have the choice to leave. I no longer believe in the fairy tale that we will live happily married ever after. Somehow it's more important just to keep the energy alive, whatever its form.

Moral Suicide

An affair destroyed Lisa's parents' marriage, an affair ended her engagement to the man she loved, and an affair ultimately threatened her own marriage. In wrestling with this chronic issue, Lisa came face-to-face with her own history, her own patterns, her own fears.

Lisa

How do you define love?

It's strange. The Eskimos have over fifty different words for snow, and the Andean Indians of South American have over three hundred kinds of potatoes. I think we need at least a hundred words to describe what we generically call love. There's passion, there's romance, there's sex, and then there's the concept that two soul mates are destined to meet and find their higher purpose. There's the love that a parent has for a child, and the love a brother has for a sister.

To me, love is an eternal and unconditional commitment to life's higher purpose, often manifest through another human being. And when we recognize that light, that truth in another human being, it awakens that love inside of us. We are mirrors for each other. When the mirror of your soul reflects the love in me, then I see the love in you. And I think that is what love is—these images, flashes, and glimpses of the love within ourselves.

We are brought up to believe in so many fairy tales—the damsel getting rescued, the prince and princess living happily ever after, etc. In my life, I have had a hard time conforming to these illusions which never rang true for me. However, I have always felt that my path was one of love. That created an unnatural contradiction for me.

Did you consider yourself to be a dutiful daughter in childhood?

I did. Decisions were made for me and I was given clear orders about how I was expected to behave and function within the family and within society. When I chose not to follow that prescribed path, I was ostracized by my family. I dared to question their formula for wealth, affluence, and success. I saw what that formula had done to many of my family members, and I decided that I did not want to be a part of it. Now we call that kind of family dysfunctional, but that term was around twenty years ago. Instead of a family that loved and supported each other, I saw brother sabotaging brother, and parents encouraging their children to compete for affection and material rewards. Relationships were based on ambition and selfishness. Family life was based on power and money, not on love. I decided that was not the way I wanted to live.

When you went your own way, did your family feel betrayed by you?
Yes, in many ways, I was regarded as a black sheep, the one who had lost her way. They were in denial that there was anything wrong with their own way of life.

In my late teens and early twenties, my parents went through a horrendous divorce. My mother was having an affair and my father was reacting out of desperation.

What do you think your mother wanted from her divorce?
She had her own reasons for divorcing my father, which I understand a lot better now than I did at the time. Back then I felt that she was trading my father in for someone else, someone she was having an affair with. Her lover had a lot of charisma, and my mother was completely charmed. She had been in a dependent relationship for years that stifled who she was. She needed to break free of all she had ever known and claim the love she thought she deserved. Still, the way in which she did it had devastating effects on us children. The divorce was a nightmare. She lied to us covertly by not telling us what was happening. She even kidnapped my younger brother and sister away from our father. I felt that she was doing what she wanted at our expense. Although I felt compassion for what my parents were going through, I felt that my life was of little importance to them. I became bitter about the whole concept of marriage.

After nearly dying in a car accident, I got the message that I had a conscious choice to make, to embrace either life or death. If I was to choose life, a lot of my self-destructive behavior patterns needed to change. I began to open up to a whole new way of being, a new way of seeing life. I studied philosophy and began to practice yoga. I became a vegetarian and quit smoking. I tried a few mind-expanding drugs and had experiences I found to be complementary to my inner growth. Since I could no longer trust in my parents and the life I had been raised to live, I had to trust that life itself would guide me and provide what I needed.

How many times have you been married?
Twice. My first marriage was extremely disillusioning; it was for romantic love, passion, and desire, but I paid a high price in terms of self-esteem. I even gave up Paul, the man I truly loved. I betrayed the very one who had opened the doors of perception for me, shown me the world of spirit, and helped me heal from the pain and trauma of my earlier years. We had shared some very wonderful years together. He constantly challenged me to grow. I took this nurturing relationship for granted. We were engaged to be married

and I had grown comfortable and secure. I assumed we would always be together. Then Scott, an old friend of his, appeared in our lives. I was moonstruck, insane with infatuation. I would do anything to be with Scott. I was so confused, I couldn't see how I could marry Paul, so I broke my engagement and ran away. Psychologically and emotionally, I went off the cliff. It was like a screenplay. I betrayed my fiancé for another man. Not only that, the other man was my fiancé's best friend. I was responsible for sabotaging my own chance for success in marriage.

I had to look at the way my mother's pattern was beginning to replay itself in my life. It was terrifying. I felt that I could not be trusted to make a commitment, afraid that I was incapable of being a loyal, truthful, and loving partner. I did eventually marry Scott and after the marriage failed, it turned me inside out. I could not forgive myself.

In the meantime, Paul married somebody else even though I knew he was still in love with me. On my way to their wedding, I decided that I was going to leave Scott. I knew I should have been the one at the altar marrying Paul.

Several years later, I was living in San Francisco, still recovering from the breakup of my first marriage, and Paul called. He was at the airport, en route home from a vacation in Guatemala. He wanted to see me. I agreed, and we ended up spending the weekend together.

Years passed. I didn't hear from him again and eventually I married my current husband, Tony. Paul recently reappeared in my life and told me that as a result of our weekend together, his wife divorced him. In the meantime, he married and divorced a second time, and has had about twenty affairs on the side. Basically, he ended up doing the same thing I had done to him twenty years ago. It all came full circle. I told him that I was sorry for what had happened, I regretted that we didn't stay together and work things out, but obviously, we both had lessons we needed to learn. He had to stop judging me for the very thing he ended up doing to all the other women he has tried to love since.

Seeing Paul again was very healing, to forgive and be forgiven for what had happened half a lifetime ago. All that time I had carried a burden of guilt for what I had done to him. It felt good to be relieved of that burden and to know that the true connection between us was of an eternal nature. I admit that there was a longing in me to re-create the past with him, but that fantasy became one more thing to let go of.

What were the circumstances of your current marriage?

Ironically, I have noticed that with all the men I love, I keep discovering the same person over and over again. Although the faces and personalities are different, in spirit, they are the same being.

When I first met Tony, I recognized the spirit in him that I had loved in Paul and in Scott. To me that was a sign that he was the one I would continue to grow with. Some people call it meeting your soul mate. Tony walked into my life shortly after my last encounter with Paul. I was at peace with myself, having recently forgiven myself for the relationships that hadn't worked out. I had made a conscious choice to get off what I called the romantic roller coaster. I was ready for that cycle of disappointment to end. I was living alone and felt ready for the real thing. I was ready to accept whatever that meant.

When I first saw Tony, there was an immediate sexual attraction, but it was different, in that I did not care whether it would worked out or not. It didn't matter if we were together a night, a day, a month, a year, or a lifetime. I felt so at home with myself that my life didn't depend on whether he was there or not. I was not entering this relationship from a place of need or desperation but I was simply making room in my life to share it with another person. That was a different approach from any other relationship I had ever had.

He was also very pure, clean, and innocent. I could see that trust and love had not been shattered in him. In many ways, I was the first woman he had ever really been in love with. He was like a virgin. I was older with much more experience, but I felt that could be dealt with.

There was a wonderful period of courtship. We took one step at a time and before long decided to start living together. I felt at peace with my past before making a commitment to him. After living together for almost a year, I discovered I was pregnant. So we decided to get married and raise a family. Although I had a lot of fears, I realized that the best way to heal the past was to have a husband and children of my own. To Tony, marriage was a sacred vow and a lifetime commitment. Because of my past, being married has been harder for me. It is very challenging, not something that comes easily. Tony has been very patient with me.

There was a sweetness and devotion in those early years when the children were born that made us very close, they were some of the happiest years of my life, although difficult.

What were you afraid of in marriage? Why was it such a challenge?
I have to answer that in a roundabout way. Initially, I didn't think that I had to be married. Other people could be married in the more conventional way. Marriage was something that I had rejected and wanted no part of, but I felt that Tony and I could have the kind of marriage in which we would be equal partners, that I could pursue my career goals without being sabotaged and controlled by my husband. Financially, I could carry my own weight, so I knew I didn't need to depend on him. I wanted to maintain my personal power and still be married.

After I had children, I found that I was expected to give up my "selfish" ideas of freedom to serve the higher institution of marriage and family life. Physiologically, the reality of nursing and caring for a child twenty-four hours a day didn't leave much time or energy for other pursuits. I felt that I was sinking into the morass of suburban life.

What do you think it means to be a good wife and mother?
From society's viewpoint, a husband and children are the most important thing in a woman's life. She is expected to surrender her needs to theirs, in a state of constant self-sacrifice. A good wife and mother puts herself last. My idea of being a good mother is to enable my children to reach their highest potential in life, to realize their goals and empower them to attain those goals. The same goes for being a good wife. I want to support my husband in his highest happiness, in being all that he can be.

How would you define a good husband and father?
According to society, a good husband provides for his family. He is the protector, the hero, the home builder, the warrior, so that his family can be safe and comfortable. That is his role. To me, a good husband is an equal partner who can share all the ups and downs, all the joys and sorrows of life without blaming me when things go wrong. A good husband appreciates my desire to participate in life beyond the front door of our home and will support me in whatever that means. Together we strive to achieve our highest potential both as individuals and as a family unit.

Because you came into your marriage with your own money and with a lot more experience, did you feel in some ways that you took on the classically male role as provider?
In many ways, that was my mother's strategy—to maintain her own financial power and independence. Without realizing it, she taught me that financial independence meant personal independence. For me, having my own money was my way of bucking the system and trying to be married in a different way. I knew I was not capable of playing the classic female role and being married in the conventional way. It was my understanding that we would both contribute to the relationship 50/50, on all levels, including the financial one. I was able to enter into partnership as an equal.

How do you feel about it now?
The drawback is that you can never truly be vulnerable and allow yourself to be taken care of. It means always being strong. I would like to be able to let go of that self-protective stance, but I don't feel that I can.

How do you think the institution of marriage would change if women were able to walk into it with their own money?
Men and women would be playing with the same deck of cards and marriage would be a lot heathier. Women would no longer have to marry for

economic dependence and could afford the luxury of marrying for other reasons. Because they have been dependent, women have had to manipulate men in order to survive. Now that women in our society are making their bid for power, marriage is becoming more of a choice than a necessity, and that has made it necessary to redefine what marriage is. I am glad to see it becoming more of a partnership and less of a contract. People are making more conscious choices out of freedom rather than economic necessity.

When you got married, did you consider yourself to be monogamous?
At the time, I certainly did. Although I have been lucky enough to experience a variety of different relationships in my life, I have always been happiest when I was deeply and spiritually committed to one man. For me, monogamy grows out of a state of being where I am so fulfilled by my partner, it wouldn't even enter my mind to get involved with someone else. To me, monogamy is something that comes from within. It's not a matter of obeying a set of rules established by some moral or religious order.

Have you had an affair during your marriage?
Once. I have been in a committed relationship with my husband for fifteen years. During that time, I fell in love with another man and had an affair that threatened to destroy my marriage. It turned my life inside out, making me examine a lot of my core issues and relive the choices my mother made. It affected my life more profoundly than any other relationship I have ever had.

Why were you attracted to him?
Our personalities are very much alike. There are certain people who understand how you think, and you understand how they think. It's easy to be together and very enjoyable. That's how Brian made me feel. At first, it was a very close friendship, but the sexual attraction was obvious from the start. His charisma and magnetism put me in a state of heightened exhilaration. It made me feel very feminine, surrendering to his masculine power. He awakened something in me that had been dormant. His love of independence was just as fierce as mine. His passion for life and sense of adventure was just as fierce, too. I was not at all prepared for how he would affect me.

Did he recognize something in you that your husband did not?
I felt that he understood things about me that my husband didn't, things I never even had to put into words. He accepted me without judgment and encouraged my growth in areas that my husband found threatening. Brian was so independent, he didn't need me in that way. Whatever I have chosen to do, he has always supported me unconditionally. He recognized me as a

free spirit and knew that is the only way I will ever be happy. He did not set any boundaries for me. It was wonderful to find an equal in so many ways.

I have often wondered what it would be like to be in a committed relationship with Brian. It could be wonderful or it could be a total disaster. I'll never know. Things usually turn out the way they do for a reason.

What gave him the ability to accept you in this way?

Because I am not his wife, he is not attached to me. If I were his wife, it would be different. He does not try to control me; he's not jealous if I interact with other men. He's not attached, so he can just let me be who I am. That has its advantages and disadvantages. Total freedom is very exhilarating, but at the same time, there is no commitment or security—the things you find in marriage.

After wrestling with this issue for years, I have realized that I need both in my life. I need the security and commitment of marriage, knowing that someone will always be there. Yet I also need the freedom, spontaneity, and creativity of a relationship that doesn't necessarily have to be sexual.

Do you think that it is easier to be in love with someone if you are not with them twenty-four hours a day?

Absolutely. I call it enjoying the whipped cream of life. But who could live on a steady diet of whipped cream? You don't have to deal with the issues of day-to-day survival. In that sense, an affair exists outside the boundaries of reality.

A woman or a man has the right to experience all these different dimensions in life and not be put in a position where the choice has to be made of one over the other. It is a tragedy when that happens. If you have a relationship with someone outside your marriage, it is traditionally called an affair. Yet really it is this other side of you that is being nourished. There may be sex involved, but in my experience sex is a minimal part of it. It is a nourishing and supportive relationship that brings out something in you that needs to live, something that makes you sparkle and shine. I think people have a right to experience that without threatening the primary relationship.

The tragedy happens when the affair is discovered and exposed. When the lovers are found out, society says, "You are allowed to love only one person, so you have to choose." If you choose one you pay one price, and if you choose the other, you pay another price. If you choose the passion and adventure of the love affair, you lose the security and continuity of the marriage. It can also damage your relationship with your children. It's a mess. Yet if you give up that creative passion that makes you feel alive and go home feeling repentant and guilty, then something in you dies—you lose the desire to love anyone. Being forced to choose can create a real tragedy. That is the dilemma as I see it.

Did your husband know about your affair?

He found out about my affair with Brian when it was at its most intense. Tony and I went away for the weekend together, and he sensed that something was going on. When he asked me about it, I had to tell him the truth. It was a major disillusionment and upheaval for him, and a critical time in our relationship. We separated for a period of time so that I could decide whether or not to end the affair. I was in a state of deep depression, and Tony couldn't bear to live with the fact that I was still seeing Brian. I decided that my family meant too much to me, so I stopped seeing Brian, and after several months, Tony and I saw each other again. We rode this roller coaster a number of times. It finally ended when Tony and I moved away for several years. We needed to give ourselves a chance to heal far away from the whole situation.

Do you think that Tony morally judged you?

Yes, I do. He saw it all as very black and white. He was innocent and I had wronged him, and somehow I ought to pay for it. That made things really hard at first. He was not able to understand the inner turmoil and chaos that I was going through. He could not support me in my pain. If anything, he thought I deserved to suffer for what I had done. That angered me, and for a long time, it alienated me even further from him.

Are you still in a relationship with Brian?

Yes, but it has changed. It was very passionate at one time. That had to end when it became dangerous and destructive. Finally, Brian decided he wanted to work things out with his wife, and I decided I wanted Tony to come back. We tried not to see each other for a while, but that didn't work either. Eventually, we found our way back into each other's lives, and now we're just good friends.

We have come to the point where we accept that what is between us is just there. We have a place in each other's lives. Sometimes it's a blessing and sometimes it's a curse. The friendship we now have is nonthreatening and seems to work well enough for everyone concerned; it has been almost ten years. It was and still is a very special relationship to me. I feel as if it exists in a world unto itself, beyond the time/space continuum. To me, real love—for anyone—lives on the eternal plane, which also happens to be a dimension beyond sex.

How have you handled the guilt?

Covering up was the hardest part for me, because by nature I am basically an honest person. I don't really know how to lie, and when I try to lie, I feel awful. Lying puts me in a state of moral suicide.

When Brian asked me to have an affair with him, he made me promise not to tell my husband. If someone found out, he said he would deny it.

Reluctantly I agreed to do it his way. At first, it was delightful to have this secret, then it began to feel like an artificial, drug-induced high that would eventually result in a crash. It began to erode my soul. But it was hard to resist the power between us. I spent the first year I knew him resisting the magnetic attraction. I never wanted to have an affair, so I denied it was even there. Finally the energy was so powerful, it was bigger than both of us. It took almost two years to unfold.

Naive as it was, I truly believed that the affair was going to take us in a positive direction. If what was between us was love, I believed that it would all work out. I remember saying a little prayer along those lines, praying that our love would bring more love into the lives of those it touched. I did not want to bring on the pain and suffering that I had experienced in my childhood. I was terrified of replaying my mother's movie. That was my nightmare. In retrospect, I was ignoring the negative, destructive side of what was unfolding, too.

Did he ever have any intention of leaving his wife?

I don't think so. I didn't want him to. I wanted him to work out his relationship with her because I knew that is what would make him happiest in the long run. It was morally acceptable for him to have an affair outside his marriage, and he could comfortably go home to her, but it was not the same for me. After a while, I could not live that two-faced life. As I got more deeply involved, I naturally withdrew my affection from my husband.

When I was with Brian at first, I had more love and energy to bring home to Tony. It seemed to make things better in my marriage, and maybe that's what Brian was doing with his wife. But after a while, it began to feel like a kind of spiritual vampirism. When I came down off the high, I would find an incredibly deep emptiness inside. I felt desperately isolated because I couldn't openly share with Tony what was going on in my life. Even after I confessed to him, I felt I had to keep everything I was feeling from my husband. I feared his anger. This kind of lying—the lie of withholding from someone you love—put me in a kind of prison.

Over time, did your feelings change about the morality of your affair?

I eventually had to admit that I was addicted to this man. My passion and desire to be with him reminded me of how being with Scott had destroyed my relationship with Paul. I couldn't believe that I had sacrificed my own morality in order for it to happen a second time.

Do you think that Brian really loves you?

One of the things I learned is that some men love selfishly. When they see a woman who is beautiful, intelligent, or wealthy, they want to capture and possess her, and dominate her. They also want to use her energy for their own self-glorification. They want to be seen with someone who looks really good. Women are capable of doing that, too. Using people is not restricted to gender.

I wanted Brian to realize his own potential to love both me and his wife. I challenged him to take that energy home and make it work with her. That is exactly what he did—especially after I asked him what kind of person he could be to even consider leaving her. In many ways, I kept sending him back home because that is where he belonged. They have grown a lot and now their marriage seems to be more solid than ever. After the pain of my own parents' divorce, I did not want to see his family go through what I had been through. I tried to love him unselfishly. If I really loved him, the greatest thing I could do was to help save his marriage.

But I still had to live with the pain of feeling taken advantage of. I felt like their healing had taken place at my expense, and now I had to put back the pieces of my life, too. Later, I realized that he was not capable of returning the healing. You can't expect someone to give what they don't have to give. He gave all that he could. There's nothing worse for a man than giving all that he can and for a woman to imply that it's not enough. So, I simply accepted what he chose to give. He appreciates me more now than at any other time in the past.

Does his wife know about his affair?

I honestly don't know. She pretends not to, but I can't imagine that someone who has been with him as long as she has and who is as intelligent as she is couldn't know. I think she knows that if she confronted him about it, he might leave, and she doesn't want to lose him.

To your knowledge, has your husband ever had an affair?

Not to my knowledge. He is by nature a monogamous person, something I really love about him. He seems to have no desire to have an affair while he is in a committed relationship. During our separation, we made an agreement that we were free to have relationships with other people if either of us wanted to without the other questioning it. So, I don't really know.

When he came back after a six-month separation, he said that he had been involved with a couple of other women. I appreciated that he had been discreet and that he completely left these other women behind when he returned home.

What is the main issue of your healing?

Healing the destruction of the trust between us. Something sacred between us had been violated. You have to remember that I was his first love. Most people go through that kind of disillusionment over their first love. I think in many ways it is a rite of passage, to experience that loss of innocence.

Does your husband trust you now?

I think he knows that I have come full circle with the whole experience. I think he accepts that it was something I needed to go through for my own growth. His greatest fear was that I would leave him, which made him look at his dependence. When he finally got to a state of detachment about whether I stayed with him or not, it actually improved our relationship. Now that he knows that he can survive without me, he can decide to be with me out of choice.

We are still working on the trust between us. It has been a long, long path. People have told me I have one of the most difficult marriages they have ever seen. It has been a difficult journey for me, but out of sheer determination we will probably stay together until death do us part.

Do you think that you will continue to push the boundaries of your marriage?

I don't regret anything that has happened. I have gained a lot of experience from this situation, which has been ten years in its unfolding. At this point, I am rather exhausted and would like some emotional stability for a while. Right now I don't feel the need to ever have another affair, especially while I am married, but who knows what the future holds?

What are the three most important things that you have learned?

The first lesson is from the well of ancient wisdom, know thyself and to thine own self be true. The second lesson is that, in spite of everything, surrender to the power of love. Trust that it will take you where you need to go and will teach you what you need to learn. Love will be ecstatically pleasurable and excruciatingly painful. Accept both and follow the flow. The third lesson is, be responsible for your actions. Be consciously aware of every decision you make and of how your actions affect the lives of others. Once you have thrown the stone in the pond, the ripples go on forever until they reach the shore.

Again, how do you define love?

Love exists when two people recognize the divine in each other and help each other fulfill their highest potential. They also accept that no one is perfect and we are all here to learn. Love is gentle and forgiving because the pain of life is inevitable.

The Inner Voice

Mike tells about a brief affair which led to his wife leaving him for one of his best friends. Although Mike admits that he and his wife might have eventually separated anyway, he still feels betrayed and disillusioned. Realizing that his marriage was not what he thought it was, Mike has been forced to find new meaning in his life. An unintentional candidate for personal growth, Mike finds himself with the opportunity to start over and have the kind of relationship he never dreamed possible.

Mike

What was your marriage like?

For years I played the role of provider. Having established a very successful chiropractic practice, I had the ability to make money. Meanwhile, Joanna devoted all her energy to being a mother and building a home. Then she got bored with it.

Did she ever want to have a career?

Yes. At first I listened to her and tried to help her figure out what she could do, encouraging her to pursue her interests. First it was real estate. She went to school, and I helped her get her license. After that she tried insurance. When she didn't like that, she went to work at a title company where they loved her. She got bored there and decided she wanted to do medical transcriptions. She took more classes and I bought all the equipment she needed. Her first day on the job, the doctor said something that offended her, so she never went back. Next, she decided she wanted to be a writer.

Why do you think she had such a hard time staying with one job?

I don't really know. All I can say is that in a career, as in a relationship, you have to be willing to work through the hard times and pay your dues. You have to struggle with it even when you want to quit. She couldn't—or wasn't willing to—do that. Maybe she was doing what she thought I wanted her to do. Due to her upbringing, she never had any practical goals. She was raised in East Coast high society and was used to having everything come easily to her. I don't think she ever really knew what she wanted.

How was your frustration affecting your relationship?

I felt that I was carrying the burden of responsibility. At one point I asked her to make an extra $500 a month so that we could live without so much financial stress, but she couldn't deal with real problems or pressing needs.

I couldn't make her do something she didn't want to do, so I supported her being a writer. She went away to writing seminars, joined a writing group, submitted a few articles, and finally got something published. Then she changed her mind and decided she wanted to be a teacher. That was it. I was at the end of my rope. I had no more patience. It meant three more years of paying tuition with no income to balance it. In the end, maybe being a teacher is what she really wanted. I only wish she had made the decision ten years earlier.

When I lost faith in her, it was the beginning of the end. I felt I was doomed to work six days a week for the rest of my life with a dependent wife rather than an equal partner. I didn't believe she would ever finish anything. I asked her to help me with my office work part-time so that she wouldn't have to work elsewhere figuring that way she would be able to spend time at home with our daughter, but she ended up hating that too.

Do you think this situation opened the door for an affair?

We talked about the issue of having affairs because her first husband had left her for another woman. She said she wouldn't tolerate it. At the time, I couldn't imagine wanting anyone else, although I had many opportunities during the ten years we had been together. However, when I became disillusioned with my life and with Joanna, something in me rebelled. Why should I be faithful and devoted while everyone else was screwing around? I was just a cog in the wheel of a big machine, someone to bring home the paycheck. I told Joanna that I felt that I was being used. I didn't feel loved; I felt I was making money only so that she could have the lifestyle she wanted.

So when this woman at work who had been after me a long time asked if I wanted to have an affair, I went for it. After a few weeks, I knew it was stupid. It was causing a disruption in my life, and it wasn't fair to me or the two women, so I broke it off.

Did you have feelings for this woman?

Yes. Part of the attraction was that Gloria admired me, making me feel like a desirable and worthwhile human being. We liked to do a lot of the same things. For example, I love to ski whereas during the ten years we were together, Joanna went skiing with me maybe three times.

How were things at home?

Because I couldn't get excited about her wanting to be a teacher, Joanna seemed to have lost her desire for me. I lost faith in her as a partner and she lost her trust in me. We were in denial about how sick our relationship had become.

When role did Chris play in your lives?
Chris and I were skiing buddies. I was his chiropractor, and he had a very successful real estate office in town. You might say we were best friends, but looking back on it, it was a weird kind of friendship. Chris could never talk about things in a direct way. There was always an undercurrent of competition between us—who could ski the fastest, catch the biggest fish, that type of thing. He thought he was always right; he had no humility.

What was the state of Chris' marriage at the time?
Not so good. He and Eve were having trouble and sometimes Chris would be very mean to her, humiliating her in front of us and abusing her in other ways, too. He was a big guy and would tease her by holding her upside down, making her feel powerless. Maybe he was already looking around for a replacement, even though he never said anything specific. I sensed that Chris had had at least one affair, probably more, behind Eve's back. I was in the middle of my affair at the time, so both of us had relationships that were on the rocks, but we never talked about our personal lives.

Do you think Chris used your friendship to get to Joanna?
I am not sure if that was his intention, but it was the end result. We didn't know each other's wives at all. Then I invited him over to meet my family. They came for dinner, he invited us to their cabin in the mountains, and it went on from there.

One evening we were having a conversation and the topic of infidelity came up. Chris said that he didn't see how his being sexually intimate with another woman would affect Eve if she didn't know about it. I couldn't believe the insensitivity and naiveté of his attitude. This was before the whole issue of AIDS became so prevalent. When Joanna heard what he said, she began to cry. She thought Chris was a complete jerk. I just thought he was a very bizarre character.

Later on, things went really sour between Chris and Eve and they were on the verge of separation. By this time, Chris was in the habit of making his weekly rounds, calling on his various women friends, and Joanna became one of them.

Why do you think she changed her mind about him?
He became a new character in her fantasy world. Because I was trying to make her face reality, she wanted out—and Chris was there ready to play hero.

Why do you think Joanna lived in such a fantasy world?

Joanna grew up in an alcoholic family, an environment where everyone pretended that everything was fine when it wasn't. As members of high society, their social code covered up the truth. Her mother wore a phony smile in the midst of chaos and calamity, while her father drank himself to death by the age of forty-five. Yet they had to maintain an image of themselves as aristocratic and superior. The only way they could do that was through denial, hiding family secrets and not communicating about feelings.

Do you think we are all victims of our upbringing?

Not necessarily. I think if you go on living without being actively conscious, you are doomed to mirror what your parents and society have projected onto you. As humans, we have the ability for self-awareness, but we also have to be willing to do the work. We can change the direction of our lives, but we have to be clear about our real issues, goals, and priorities.

In what way was Joanna unwilling to change?

She had no real negotiating skills whatsoever. Rather than learning how to negotiate with another human being in a partnership, she would comply only on the surface, or give up and retreat into her fantasy life.

When Chris sensed Joanna's unhappiness, he moved in as her confidant. Being the rescuer was the perfect role for him. As a result, Joanna didn't have to work on our relationship. Chris would call Joanna all the time, and Eve began to get suspicious. Finally, she was convinced they were having an affair, and that's why she left Chris.

Did you say anything to Chris?

After Eve left, Chris kept coming over to the house alone. I asked him to find a woman friend so that we could do things together again as couples. Four seemed like a better balance than this constant threesome.

Joanna kept talking to Chris about our personal problems, and not to me. That really hurt. Our personal life was none of his business. I finally asked him to leave us alone for a while so that we could work things out ourselves. I guess he and Joanna continued seeing each other anyway.

We could never really talk about it because Chris denied that there was anything romantic between them, and so did she. Chris called it a friendship. I think that Joanna instinctively knew about the affair I had with Gloria years earlier. To her, that justified whatever she was doing with Chris. And because they weren't actually sleeping together, she thought I had no right to complain.

I finally said, "So you are celibate lovers—what's the difference? It doesn't matter whether you're screwing or not. What bothers me is that you feel more for him than you feel for me. It's a basic shift in the energy between us, and it's changing the dynamics of our marriage." She still wouldn't talk about it. She insists that they never made love until she moved out last year. Two weeks after she left me, he moved in with her.

When did you first feel her slipping away?
It began when we were first married. When we had our daughter, things got better for a while. Having a family really pulled us together. But when we lost another baby, it really killed something inside her.

Did you feel you were doing more for the marriage than she was?
Superficially, she put the decorative touches on our life to make it look like the perfect family, but she was not really there emotionally. We became more disconnected every year. My affair was the final nail in the coffin, destroying any trust she had left for me.

Did the truth about your affair ever come out?
It has been my experience that when you are in a relationship, an intuitive woman knows about it. There's no way you can prevent it. She just knows. I think that she felt it but didn't say anything to me. When Joanna confronted me, I found it easy to deny it because it was already over.

Was denying it a mistake?
With a different woman it would have been, but with Joanna it was not a mistake. I knew how she felt about it: she would have left me immediately. She would not have understood or tried to work things out. I think she was looking for an excuse to leave. I thought the only way to save my marriage was to close the door on my affair. I wanted to put as much time and distance between me and the affair as possible before I had to admit it. I went on with life as if it had never happened. I was in denial too. I just wanted to save us.

How did the affair change your attitude toward your marriage?
I think when people have an affair, they can go one of two ways. They can give up and go on to the next relationship, and probably repeat the same mistake—or they can really begin to love the person they are with. That is what happened to me. After I acted out my disillusionment, I decided that the affair, the sex, and the excitement were not what I wanted. All I wanted was a family and a partner I could work on long-range goals with. I wanted to be with someone who would love me even if I made a mistake, someone I could talk to about it. I craved the feeling of being loved and admired. I tried to find these things with Joanna. I told Joanna I wanted to go to couple's counseling and work on some of these issues so we could bring it all out in the open. Four years after the fact, I finally admitted that I had an affair. I told her I had lied because I was afraid she would leave me. I apologized and asked her not to

hate me. Instead of forgiving me, she was very angry and went straight to Chris in self-righteous indignation. She didn't understand my side of it at all.

She said that she had stopped loving me years ago. I asked her why she had stayed with me all these years. She said it was because I could give her the life she wanted. I was the paycheck, and she felt that she was prostituting herself. Any further counseling seemed pointless.

Is that why she left?

We finally admitted to each other that we couldn't do it anymore. I wasn't sleeping at night. I couldn't invest any more energy into a relationship she didn't want or believe in. As soon as she was sure Chris would take care of her, she left.

Why do you think she fell out of love with you?

It was a slow process of realizing that we were different people with different goals. I don't think that she was a whole person, a person capable of being an equal partner. As much as she wants to believe that she is a feminist, she wasn't trained to do anything, and she didn't have the determination to start something of her own. Joanna and I had been moving in different directions for quite a while. We didn't have a shared vision of what we wanted our family life to be.

Did she leave because of your affair?

Yes, but I still don't think that is sufficient grounds to leave. People are not perfect. Things happen. If you're married to somebody, you're married to a human being, not a machine.

Do you think you had more to learn by losing your marriage than by saving it?

I think I had more to learn by having the affair and having the problem, but if we had saved our marriage, that too would have been an incredible learning experience and an opportunity to grow. Our marriage would have been stronger than many other marriages. We could have reestablished a spiritual connection. I might have even been able to accept her feelings for Chris, but she wasn't willing to go any further.

Can you describe your disillusionment over being betrayed by both your wife and your best friend?

I can't tell you how much anger and pain I feel toward Chris. It is probably so buried and so deep that I can't even begin to get in touch with it. If I did, it would probably be harmful. I don't think I will ever completely forgive him for his deviousness. I think there's a certain part of him that thrives on the wounds of others. A true friend would have told Joanna to go home and figure out her problems with me. Even though Chris came into it believing he was a good guy, I think he took advantage of the situation for his own benefit.

As for Joanna, when things got really messed up, I don't think she knew how to ask for help. I tried to get her into counseling, but she wasn't willing to work on it.

Did Chris just catalyze an inevitable process?

Often I wonder, if Chris hadn't been there, would there have been someone else? Or would Joanna have opened up to me and worked it out? Maybe we would have patched things up for a while and then broken up five or ten years later. Who knows? But I am still angry at Chris because I feel he let me down as a friend. I don't think I will ever respect or trust him again.

He has probably done me a favor by taking Joanna off my hands. Eventually, I won't have to support her anymore, and now I have an opportunity to have a relationship with somebody who really wants me. Someday I will probably thank him.

Has your experience with Joanna affected your ability to trust women?

It has affected my ability to depend on women and to trust that they mean what they say, but I am sure that all women are not that way. Maybe my cynicism is just protecting me. I have to admit that my marriage to Joanna was a bad relationship with serious problems. It would have taken a tremendous amount of work to save it.

I believe that until we look honestly at our script in life, until we look at our mistakes of the past, we are doomed to repeat them. In retrospect, I have to admit that I was addicted to my wife. I wouldn't let go, even when I knew that to stay with her was destroying me.

What regrets do you have if any?

I wish I had called someone for help when I was first feeling cynical, before I got involved with my affair. I would have had more integrity. Having an affair is a really public way to make a mistake, and it really embarrassed me. It was hell for my self-esteem.

Where are you in your own healing process?

It's getting easier to talk about all this because I am feeling better and better about being alone. Nine months after Joanna left, I felt a major sense of relief. I am still very attached to my daughter and concerned for her welfare.

I am the type of person who likes to bond, who likes to share my life with another person. As human beings, I think that family life is essential for spiritual growth. So what do I do—look for someone to fit into my dream? Or do I remodel my dream to fit a new kind of relationship? Can I ever trust someone again to be my partner?

I really don't know the answers to these questions. Joanna's leaving set me back in my life plan at least ten years, but I would rather lose her now than ten years down the road. It still gives me the hope of creating something new.

If you had it all to do over again, what would you do differently?
I would never have married Joanna. No, I don't really mean that. I got a lot of good things from the relationship, especially my daughter. I thank God for her.

Do you think that history will repeat itself with Joanna and Chris?
I hope not, because I don't want to see my daughter get hurt again. I wish Joanna and Chris the best.

What do you think now of having affairs?
Having an affair is not all that it is made out to be. To me it's a symptom of a sick life. Affairs probably hurt everyone involved, including those having the affair as well as the ones who are being betrayed. I know that I will never have another affair. Now the idea of it is not even attractive to me. I ended up hating the woman I had the affair with, because of her dishonesty and her unwillingness to let go of it. It's not love. It's very selfish.

How do you feel about someone else who is having an affair?
If I have a friend who is having an affair, I will make sure he doesn't interact with my family. Chris injured me after I opened my home to him, and I don't think I'll ever trust another guy to come that close to my family again. He violated a taboo that exists so that we don't kill each other. Taboos are old tribal laws that were established for the survival of the tribe. One of them is: if you come into my tent as my friend, don't steal from me.

What did your inner voice tell you about Chris?
One time he was bragging to me about how much money he was going to make and how successful his business was going to be. I heard that little voice inside say, "My family is not for sale," but I think it was, and Joanna sold it to him. She wanted what he had to offer. Chris wanted a ready-made family and he got mine. For her to sell herself to him tells me that she was never really connected to me in a spiritual way. It makes me realize that our marriage was never anything more than a financial arrangement.

One of the hardest things for me to admit is that I did not have a clear picture of who my wife really was and what she was capable of. When I look back on our relationship, so much of it was fantasy. When we broke up, I lost my dream, that our careers would blossom together and that we would build a beautiful home and have a loving family, the dream that we were something special. Letting go of that dream has been harder than anything else.

The Myth of Marriage

Jason has gone one hundred percent into every relationship he has ever had including five marriages and five divorces. Many miles down the road of life, Jason reflects on what the essence of an affair is, what a marriage is and who he is in relation to both.

Jason

In light of your experience, to what degree do affairs work or not work in the context of marriage?

Love is the theme running through it all. You have to wonder if self-love or love for the other person is really the issue here: are you after what you want, or are you responding to the other person's wants and needs? For me, it has usually been a mutual recognition that has been instantly felt by both beings. That spark is there, that connection is there; it cannot be denied, although it can't always be fulfilled at that moment. Just the recognition of it is usually sufficient. You can even let it go. You don't have to follow through on every spark, but then again there aren't that many. You don't fall in love with everybody—only certain people attract you.

I have loved a lot of people, but not always sexually. Nancy and I went to high school together. She was eighteen and I was nineteen when we got married. For the first five or six years, we were monogamous. We had two children and our focus was on the home, building a family, and attending college.

I was working for the city government in a job I didn't like. I had a terrible relationship with her parents and was tired of having them make decisions for us. I wanted to break away, and I asked Nancy to come with me when I got a job elsewhere, but she refused to give up the security of her home town and her parents who lived six blocks away. So I began to look elsewhere. Nancy had already tried to kill herself, and so had I. The tension and frustration of living near her parents were unbearable. They were there all the time, telling us what to do. She and the kids were hooked so deeply into this lifestyle, I couldn't dislodge them, and I knew I couldn't take it any more.

How did your first affair take place?

I was just being a good daddy, taking care of my kids in the back yard, while my wife and her mom were out shopping. The lady next door leaned over the fence and smiled, and we started talking. We just kept on talking, and every day she leaned over the fence a little further until she fell into my arms. The next thing I knew we were making love in her apartment. I found out later that she had made a bet with some of her women friends that she could seduce me. She had heard me say that I had no interest in having affairs with other women and therefore had decided to accept the challenge—I took the bait. This woman was refreshing and free, in contrast to the intense claustrophobia I felt in my marriage. But the affair was very brief: we got together only two or three times and that was it. However, those occasions opened me up to the recognition that my marriage was dead.

I told Nancy that I was going through a crisis about our marriage and wanted to go to the mountains alone for four days and nights to sort things out. While I was up there, I got very quiet, very empty, and very clear. I realized that I had no alternative but to leave. Since Nancy and the kids didn't want to move, I had to extricate myself from the situation or we would all go crazy.

I moved out and got divorced. I was twenty-seven years old and wasn't particularly looking for anybody else. I was happy just being me for a while. In truth, I was terrified of being single again and stepping out into the world of free-flowing sexuality.

I started teaching as a college professor and met Melissa. This was in the mid-sixties, and we took LSD together. For me, the acid experience was one of pure love. I was convinced that she was divinely meant for me, that we were soul mates, but it wasn't the same for her. She had an entirely different experience and didn't realize how deeply I had fallen in love with her, but we continued to see each other. When I took a sabbatical to write a book, she moved to the country with me. We lived together in a committed relationship, as if we were married. She even used my name. We had many spiritual experiences together and got very close. When we moved back to the city a year later, after I had finished my book, I resumed teaching and she decided to become a belly dancer. I didn't mind because I liked to play the music that went with it. Melissa became a very good belly dancer and started to work at various clubs around town. She started having affairs and would bring her lovers home to meet me, an awkward situation since most of them were musicians I really respected. It was a double bind because I loved their music but I loved Melissa too. I had to learn to handle that kind of jealousy and anguish.

When I got another teaching job somewhere else, I asked her to move with me, and she said she wanted to stay. When I said I was going no matter what, she changed her mind and came with me, but it wasn't long before she whirled away with one of her lovers. So, that was Wife Number Two. Psychologically, it was like getting divorced, since we had been together for three years.

How did you get involved with your third wife?

I wasn't particularly looking for the next relationship which just emerged. For me, that is the way it has usually happened. I told Maria right away that I wasn't interested in a steady, ongoing, monogamous relationship. After my previous two experiences, I wanted a blend of both—a committed marriage that had the freedom of an affair. Of course, that approach to a relationship just doesn't work, but at least I learned much more quickly this time.

Maria got pregnant. I felt honor bound to care for the baby though we had been together only six months and I knew the relationship was already deteriorating. The first year was ragged all the way through and we shredded fast. By the time our son, Sam, was over a year old, Maria was emotionally gone and I was taking care of him whenever I wasn't teaching. Family life didn't work for us, but I loved being a father.

During the second year, we went on a trip together during my sabbatical and fought all the way. While we were traveling, Maria decided that she wanted to become a woman of the world. She started having affairs everywhere we went. When she had an affair in Turkey, she almost got herself killed. It's a Moslem society and strictly taboo for a woman to exhibit any kind of infidelity whatsoever. At one point, the chief of police called me in and said, "Either get her out of here, or she'll be dead." By the end of the trip, there was no question that it was all over with us. We separated and I kept Sam.

Do you think that she was having these affairs in reaction to the rules you had established at the beginning of your relationship?

I think that is quite possible. After she got pregnant, she didn't want to have an open marriage, and I didn't either, but the pattern was already established. One little indiscretion on my part triggered the affair syndrome again, and on our world trip she got even with me by having these flagrant affairs.

After this, how did you feel about having affairs?

It still seems to me that you have to honor the spark that exists between two people. If the spark isn't in the place where it's supposed to be, and you find it someplace else, then you have to go where it is. I have to follow the energy and be true to my heart. Often that spark is a professional connection having to do with literature or music; it doesn't always have to have a sexual context.

Throughout all of this, I had been experiencing a spiritual awakening and mind expansion. My love life often reflected what was happening in my spiritual life; my new partners were also my teachers, and together we went through tremendous change and growth. How can you be compassionate, open, and loving and *not* fall in love?

After your third marriage, what did you want in your next relationship?

I said I would never get married again and I was in transition when I met Kate, who was destined to become Wife Number Four. I was a single father and she was a single mother. She had a daughter, Rosie. We began to live together with all our children; we weren't married but we were monogamous. Kate had told me something was wrong with her reproductive system and she couldn't have any more kids. You can imagine our surprise when we found out that she was pregnant. Since we had been living together successfully, we decided that we could embrace another child in our lives.

There's something I call father's ecstasy that is the fulfillment of the sexual cycle. The sexual process starts with that first spark, that seed, and it ends with that baby in your hands. It is a very powerful cycle that goes around, and once you have been a part of it, your life has changed. It is a deepening of love that goes beyond sex.

I was in the midst of a child custody battle with Maria over Sam. She wanted him, but Kate and I felt it was better that he stay with us; she was willing to be Sam's stepmother. On some level, I was trying to re-create the family I had lost in my first marriage. Kate and I worked on that goal for about three years, and eventually even got married. Our marriage was exclusive, which to me seems both appropriate and necessary when there are children involved. I never really had a problem with that. That bonding came naturally.

But the pressures from the outside were tremendous, especially from Maria, who was determined to sabotage what we were trying to establish. When she lost the custody case, Maria decided she was going to destroy us through Sam. So he became the living seed of destruction in my marriage to Kate. It was terrible. After three years of crisis after crisis and hours and hours of family counseling, with Sam getting expelled from school after school, it all came apart. Kate and I had different ways of dealing with our lives when those crises came up, and our ways were often not compatible. When the pressures came down, we found we couldn't work them out together.

We had been monogamous with each other all the way. Then Kate got pregnant again, prompting a new crisis, because we were not doing well in our marriage and questioned if we could bring another child into the picture. She told me that she had decided to abort the baby, because she didn't see any future in our marriage. I started thinking about it and realized that I didn't want any more kids, having had four children by three different wives, so I made my decision to have a vasectomy. Kate got the abortion and was very angry with me. When we went to New Mexico on a vacation, she decided she wanted to stay there. I went home because I liked the stability of my home and my job. While we were separated, I ran into a woman I had dated before I knew Kate, and we had another brief fling. After that one night, I knew it was over with Kate. When Kate came back, she guessed immediately that I had slept with somebody. She knew it was over too.

After the failure of your fourth marriage, were you more disillusioned than ever?

By that time, I knew that the idea of monogamous love was a big joke— for me. I can look around and see that it *is* what we are expected to do, and I applaud it whenever I see it work. Do bear in mind that starting with the third marriage and all the way through the fifth, I was a nondenominational minister and performed over a hundred weddings. In my heart, I obviously do believe in marriage, I do believe in love. It is only this sacrament of love that has kept me running.

However, of all my marriages, I think the fifth was the dumbest. I still wonder why I did it, but now I think I understand why. There is a part of me that is an enabler, that wants to save people. Wife Number Five, Cherie, was a student of mine twenty years ago and had an obsession about marrying me ever since. Back then, Cherie was in the middle of divorcing her first husband and wanted to date me, but much to her distress, I ended up dating her girlfriend. Apparently, she had this longing to be with me that she was determined to fulfill. Right after I split up with Kate, she showed up in my life again when we ran into each other at church. We talked a few times. Then we went out for coffee, then we went out for breakfast—twenty-four hours later.

We started dating. But I told her that I was also dating three other women, none of them very often or very much. I didn't want to get involved in another exclusive relationship. I was enjoying my freedom.

How did Cherie persuade you to marry her?

She moved in on a rainy, stormy night in the dead of winter. She was visiting at my house and didn't want to go home because she was living in a cramped trailer in a sleazy, run-down trailer park. After I let her stay one night, she wanted to stay for another and another. I let her try it for a week. That week grew into two months, and before I knew it she was living there. She even had her own closet.

When she suggested that we get married, I asked her why she wanted to ruin a good thing. She had already been married three times. We should have both known better.

What do you think happens when an affair turns into a marriage?

I can speak only from my own experience. The truth is that each person is infinitely deep and wonderful. If we could just look beyond the ego issues, we could continue to appreciate each other indefinitely. First there's the honeymoon period when you agree to focus on each other exclusively. That's when you learn the most about each other. You have the opportunity to exchange the experiences of your respective lifetimes while the feelings are still fresh. Staying open is the key to keeping the passion of an affair in a marriage. When you get married, both partners must find a way to stay open and keep that spark alive.

Marriage brings security, and along with that certain habits and patterns of behavior settle in. I see so many long-term marriages in which both people have completely closed the doors to each other. They may live in the same house, but the rooms are empty; they walk past each other as if the other one isn't there. They simply don't relate. They may be sharing the bills and the kids, but they are not sharing their lives. We get into marriage and take each other for granted. We stop giving each other that devoted attention everyone needs. And I have been as guilty as anyone else.

How did your relationship with Cherie change after you were married?
Cherie had a good counseling job; she looked and acted as if she was on top of things. I bought the illusion that she had her life together, until I agreed to marry her, after we had been living together six months. On the day of our wedding, I knew we were in trouble. As we were getting up that morning, she forbade me to smoke. She had never mentioned a word about it before. I felt as if I had been set up and manipulated into doing something that I really didn't want to do, but I went through with it. The wedding was big and beautiful, and I was able to invite a lot of friends. I had never been able to do that before. The honeymoon was pleasant enough, too.

After we got married it all started to change. In a few months, she started nagging and manipulating me. First she quit one job, then she quit another. Before long, I was not only supporting her but her son as well, in addition to my other children. I felt that she was not honoring the agreement we had made about mutual support. She also became extremely jealous of any attention I gave the children and demanded all of my time. Cherie's attitude changed from being wonderful and accommodating to controlling and manipulative. And she needed a lot more sexual attention than I had to offer. So after a year of marriage we began two years of counseling, and went through four different counselors. By the time of the last counselor, I knew that I had enough, and I asked her to move back to the trailer park.

How did that leave you feeling?
For the next six months I was solitary. How many marriages can crash and burn before you have to ask if maybe the problem is inside yourself? I had to find out what it was about me that kept attracting women I could not stay married to. I have yet to come up with an answer.

How are your relationships with your children and your ex-wives now?

All the kids like each other. Now that I am no longer married, I still have friendly relationships with all my former wives, even Maria. Ironically, Kate has moved back into my house with our teenage daughter, Rebecca. Although our relationship is no longer sexual, it has worked well for all of us to live together, especially for Rebecca. We are more like roommates.

To work it out takes a lot of patience and a lot of love, especially when children and ex-wives are involved. Relationships take a lot of energy, and I have found that I need my creative energy for my work. I have learned how to protect myself and draw very clear boundaries that define how much I am willing to share with another person.

I have also noticed that my sexual drive has slowed down since I had my vasectomy, which makes me realize how much my life was propelled by testosterone when I was younger. It has freed me in a lot of inner ways that are much more satisfying and much less driven by the urge for sex. Sex is the ultimate creative force. So if you are an artist, you have got to keep some of that energy reserved as sacred. It's your creative juice.

I have retired from full-time dating. Now I don't even answer the phone while I am working. I am having a long-term relationship with my first love, the muse of my art.

Who has been the love of your life?
I don't know that I have ever really been in love—maybe with Wife Number Two since we bonded so deeply in our psychedelic experience, but that bonding was not mutual.

The real love of my life happened that day I opened up to the realization of what God was, and that had nothing to do with being a woman or a man, nothing at all. Sex is part of it, but sex is not what love really is, and I have never been confused about that.

Do you see romantic love as just a dance of expectation and illusion?
No. Because each time that spark happens, there is a heart-to-heart connection. That is not illusion, that is real. But it is transitory, because it keeps changing. Love is real, but it may shift the object of its focus.

Why do you think we as humans try to control love and give it a form that is stable and consistent like marriage?
Marriage is the corporate production-line concept that we were sold about a hundred years ago in America. It's an idea that was mass-produced, but like most mass-produced stuff, it doesn't work. It breaks down fast and does not come with a warranty. Even television tries to create a pervasive cultural consciousness that molds us into certain behavioral patterns. It's easier to manipulate and control people when they conform to these images. We have been given a set of expectations in our culture that says a man and

woman have to stay together exclusively until death do us part. It's the marriage paradigm and I say that it's inadequate because it doesn't cover the multiplicity of human situations or human needs. But there is also the genuine human need for nesting and creating families that has been with us for as long as the human species. That instinct is the true basis for marriage in my opinion.

Culturally, how can we deal with the disillusionment when we find out that paradigm is not true?

First of all, it is important to talk about these things, and to write books such as this one. People have to understand that the problem is with the paradigm, not with them. Monogamy is the ideal, but reality is what surrounds us.

Do you think that there is a certain type of person suited to marriage and a certain type of person suited to having an affair?

I believe that anybody is the type to have an affair. It just takes the right time, the right place, the right spark, the right mood, and the right moment. Adults are adults, and they do what they do. That's why it's called adultery.

If a married person is having an affair, do you think it is a sign that the marriage is in trouble?

Not necessarily, but it is a sign that individual is not getting what he or she needs in the relationship. Sometimes it's just a matter of appetite. Some people like a lot of spice, and some don't. Appetites vary from day to day and from person to person. It all comes down to desire. Different people have different capacities for love. Some people need an exclusive focus, while others need a more expansive one. It's not even a matter of gender but more a matter of personality. For the people who want to expand, holding back will eventually damage them. For people who want to be exclusive, having an affair will destroy them.

What is your advice to people on handling the inevitable winds of change when they blow through life?

Just the same thing I would say to someone sitting in the middle of a hurricane: hang on and pay attention. Everything that happens is an effect you have caused. When something goes wrong, figure it out and learn how not to do it again. When you understand that law of cause and effect, you can master your destiny.

How would you apply that advice to yourself in terms of marriage?

Three times I said I would never get married again, and I went and did it again. So I am not going to do that anymore. There's no need for it, especially since I am not going to have any more kids.

What is your advice to a woman who finds out that her husband is having an affair?

First of all, don't feel that you have failed. Have the courage to confront him about what is happening. Don't pretend and don't deny what is going on—not even for a day. Denial turns into poison and self-hatred.

What if she's afraid of losing him?

She needs to examine her own basis of security and ask herself why she is afraid. She's already lost him if that's the case. If she is making her husband the foundation of her life, then she is in trouble—that's probably why he is out having an affair.

Conversely, what is your advice to a man who finds out his wife is having an affair?

It's the same advice. When I found out my partner was having an affair, I felt a terrible sense of loss, anger, and guilt. The anger was not at her but at myself for having been inadequate. Finally I stopped blaming myself. We are all inadequate because no one person can be the whole universe.

One time I was driving through a neigborhood in Daly City, a tacky suburb outside of San Francisco. As I was driving down a street with identical houses lined up in a row, I noticed that all the men were out in the front driveway waxing and polishing their cars, the way they did every weekend. And they were all on the verge of divorce. I thought for a moment, if they spent as much time every week rubbing their wives as they did rubbing their goddamn cars, maybe they would have good marriages.

The question is, "Do you love her for who she is including her affair, or do you love her in relation only to you? Is she just your possession that someone is trying to steal?" It's an important question because if you are being selfish in trying to hold onto her, maybe you need to let her go. She has the right to be happy.

When an affair is happening, both sides have to realize that it might mean the end of the relationship. That's why people get so scared. The moment the affair happened, that *was* the end of the relationship as an exclusive arrangement. Something changed. Then you have to ask yourselves, "Do we still love each other? Can we live with this or go beyond it?"

What is your advice to someone dealing with the end of a relationship, accepting that it is over?

Seek counseling and friendship, and take care of yourself. Every day means letting go, and what you are letting go of is pain and illusion. In reality, that pain and illusion are over, and all you are grieving for is the attachment to both. It's just an identity crisis.

Have you always been honest with your wives about the affairs that you have had?

Eventually. Once it might have been better if I had lied, but usually I suffered more guilt from lying than I did from the affair itself. That's the truth about lying.

As a writer, I can often be creative with the way I present the truth. Sometimes in the past I was confused about my real motives, but usually my wives could tell immediately I was having an affair. Kate knew the moment I walked in the door. As a person, I have a hard time telling the truth. It's easier for me to lie.

If you had it all to do over again, what would you do differently?

When I was seventeen, I had a chance to go to Argentina and look for diamonds, but I passed on it since I had a date that weekend with a pretty girl, Nancy, and I ended up marrying her. If I had it to do over again, I would have gone to Argentina. Of course, I would have had a completely different life, and I might have been dead by the age of nineteen.

Everything was worth it just to have my children, the most wonderful things that have ever happened to me. If everything is cause and effect, then I have caused some things to happen, the results of which I love, and if I love all my children how could I not love their mothers? In truth, I wouldn't have my life any other way. I must have intuitively known that diamonds were not my best friend.

Are you an incurable romantic?

Probably, but hopefully I am cured of the need to get married.

The Open Marriage

Geoffrey and Ilse had the classical open marriage, based on the mutual agreement that they would be open to sexual relationships with other partners, with no secrets. Geoffrey's passionate affair with Emily blew the lid off. An intensely emotional and creative woman, Emily opened new doors to his inner world. Geoffrey's desire to explore this realm of personal growth eventually turned his life inside out and gave him the opportunity to discover what "open" really means.

Geoffrey

What was your motivation for wanting an open marriage?

People are constantly growing. In a relationship, you have two individuals who share common goals. Being involved with someone else doesn't threaten that shared path. In fact, it adds to it.

Ideally, my partner helps me achieve my goals, whether that means a better social life, a more successful business, or a happier family. As human beings, we find success because we work with other human beings. In a marriage, it works in a similar way. We are two individuals working in a partnership dedicated to our mutual growth.

The problem with classical western love as it has evolved is the expectation that it is supposed to last forever. Now that we have been liberated by the pill and other modern technology, we have more choices which bring on greater challenges and more threats to our stability. So here we are—faced with the continued, ever-expanding opportunity for personal growth.

With so many inviting choices, it is all too easy to realize that your partner is not growing in the same direction, especially when you feel you've already learned what you need to learn from that person. So, at any time you can ask yourself: "Is it time to move on yet? I've learned what I need to learn with you. Now I want to find someone who will help me with my next lesson." Of course not. Most of us aren't so cruel and reckless as to abandon someone who has been a long-time partner and friend, especially in marriage, but that inner conflict, that restless urge is still there. Instead of abandonment, there are alternatives. For me, it is an ongoing process of raw personal honesty, particularly in the face of a society whose rules are often based on hypocrisy and denial.

When people change and need to move on, we often judge this as failure. Yet I see these individuals as actually growing up. In my growth path, I want to experience all I can in one lifetime, and include all the possible and positive experiences that reflect my expanding dimensions. When a dynamic opportunity is there, I don't want to deny it. What we tend to judge so severely as a failure in relationship is actually a success, just like graduating.

Would you say that people outgrow each other?
I think that the mutual path a couple is on, the subconscious deal they have struck in their partnership, may have outlived its dynamic meaning. If it is mutually unfulfilling, then a dramatic change is necessary even if it means separating.

What if this awareness is not mutual?
We all have different perceptions of love, but what matters is a healthy balance between our real needs and our dreams. We need to do this while respecting the agreements we make, emotionally, subconsciously and literally.

Do you think it's possible to refine those agreements in the form of vows?
Yes and no. When it comes down to it, the vows don't really mean anything. What really means something are the day-to-day feelings you have—those are the real vows which are renewed every minute. They are absolutely real. The rest are just symbolic externalizations, which often reflect a decaying set of social rituals.

Would you say "love" as a noun is an idealistic projection—like an altar in our minds?
As a noun, it implies that love is static, and in my mind it isn't. It is dynamic, moving, and changing. Experiencing intense romantic love is not only a beautiful feeling, it is also a dramatic agent for change and personal growth.

Can you describe how your marriage shifted from a monogamous one to an open one?
It's strange, because it came as a surprise. It was not a plan at all. Instead, it was a process of discovery. The first time it happened, I got involved with someone for a brief time while my mate was in Europe. It was a short-lived affair, but it was very exciting. She prompted a realization of what I needed more of—in contrast to a safe, cookbook family life.

Can you describe the other relationship that opened the door for you?
There are a lot of things about my relationship to Emily that are still mysterious to me. At first I thought the affair would be a delightful and

enriching discovery. What surprised me was how for the first time this experience of love had blossomed to the point where I felt it was beyond my control. The feelings became so strong that I was willing to sacrifice more and more, regardless of my other commitments including my work. I would abandon whole days in the office just to be with her; I would disappear, come back four hours later and try to cover up the fact that I had been missing. There was something particularly special, powerful, and mysterious, that I have never felt for any other woman. Every moment I spent with her was more important than anything else. To my amazement, every day brought new heights to our already ecstatic passion and new depths to our profound intimacy. It was like an addictive drug for both of us.

But I also have a sense of loyalty that is even stronger than my sense of romantic love. My loyalty is a pillar, a foundation of who I am, so being disloyal to Ilse prompted a conflict, even though I could see that the goals of our relationship were increasingly out of alignment.

Emily was the catalyst that triggered my need to leave Ilse. I saw that I had been supporting her dreams to have a family but not fulfilling my own dreams.

How did you maintain your marriage throughout that time?

It was difficult, but I was able to manage. It was okay with Ilse; she knew about Emily. I wanted to be with Emily, but I also felt I needed to support Ilse emotionally.

I kept asking myself: What should I do? Fulfill obligations by doing what I am supposed to do or shut that out entirely and say, "I want to be with my lover, and that's it." I kept reassuring Ilse that the affair with Emily wasn't threatening our marriage or our long-term goals.

How did you work out the agreement to have an open marriage with Ilse?

It's a fascinating puzzle that I had to understand and work out myself. I'll give you an illustration. In the Scandinavian countries when people have affairs, which they often do, they are surprisingly candid about it. If someone asks a woman, "Where is your husband?" She may say, "Oh, he's next door with the neighbor tonight." There is nothing implied or scandalous about it. People are more inclined to discuss feelings rather than morality.

In southern Europe, it is very different. That is where people have secret affairs. There is an unwritten rule. You never breach discretion. Never. You will go to a party with a married couple, and perhaps the lover will be there. Everyone will know, but no one will a say a thing. It's very bewildering to see this scene.

Why do you believe this taboo exists?

A lot of what we do socially is based on the past. I believe that earlier cultures created strict rules of social order out of a need for stability and predictability. When someone breaches that social order, everyone gets upset. For example, in ancient provincial Japanese society, if a couple had sex before marriage, they would beat the man to death and drown the woman. It doesn't make sense for any reason other than it threatened their social order, which they saw as a higher priority.

What was the relationship between Ilse and Emily like?

Emily was unwilling to even acknowledge Ilse, which was a serious thorn in the relationship. Ilse wanted to make a connection with Emily; she wanted to know who she was and get acknowledgment from her. Emily couldn't handle that. She wouldn't even look Ilse straight in the eye, she would turn away when she ran into her at the grocery store. Naturally, Ilse felt very alienated and insulted. She couldn't understand why Emily wouldn't deal with the situation.

Perhaps Emily felt that she was competing with Ilse for you. This seems contrary to the whole concept of an open marriage, which implies sharing.

This particular aspect of my affair with Emily bothered me a lot. I really wanted Emily to grow, to see the bigger picture. I think she was afraid of confronting her inner self.

What happened between you and Ilse?

There was a growing problem between us. The kids were becoming more important to her than anything else—more important than me, than us, and even more important than her own well-being. Right now, she has been allowing the kids to destroy her; she has created what is popularly called a co-dependent relationship with them. She desperately wants to be needed. She believes so strongly in this so-called liberal upbringing that the kids have no guidelines, no rules, and so our family life became total chaos. It took four hours to put them to bed. She didn't get to sleep until past midnight and then was up at six in the morning. That didn't include the nightly whining for water and the bad dreams. She became completely unavailable to me, and she blamed me that her life was so chaotic.

Neither of us was happy. I wasn't happy about what was going on with her and the kids, and she wasn't putting any energy into the marriage. We found ourselves communicating less, becoming more divided, and we finally found ourselves tied in an inflexible knot. After twenty years, it was hard for me to undo my commitment to Ilse, to breach the trust we had created. But it was necessary and I ended the marriage.

How did it end with Emily?

I realized that what she wanted was to be saved, emotionally, to get married and be dependent on a man who was financially secure. That's not the kind of relationship I wanted. Ultimately, she wanted to be rescued from herself. I think that our relationship was a kind of test to validate her ability to love. I think that her next stage was to settle down and live a more conventional and "normal" life that matched the values she was raised with.

The breakup began when I discovered that she was lying to me about Jared, the man whom she later married. She denied that she was sleeping with him, even when I confronted her. She began to invalidate our relationship by denying our experiences and covering up our past. Then she turned on me completely; she started lying to others about us and saying negative things about me. Then she stopped keeping our dates or returning my phone calls.

The dishonesty and denial were the beginning of the end. She said later that she had been lying to me about everything—for three years. She acted as if nothing had happened, that she felt nothing and didn't want to feel anything. Once I confronted her about her behavior and there was a melodramatic scene. It was ugly.

Unfortunately, the way things ended has made it impossible for us to be friends. I decided that I didn't want to be involved with someone that manic and unstable.

Did you experience a sense of loss when things did not work out with Emily?

I don't expect to experience in my life again what I felt for Emily. I really don't. Every moment we shared was very intense. Even though the affair ended badly, I still grew a lot. Years later, I still think about her. I was surprised by how much I missed her, in spite of her faults. We occasionally cross paths, but she won't look at me. The energy between us is apparently too intense for either of us to deal with, so we say nothing.

Are you currently involved in a relationship?

Yes, and it's really fine. We are alike in many ways, easygoing yet strong willed. We drink, we cook, we eat, we make love—and we do all of that over and over again, to no end. Every night we make romantic settings with candlelight, music, and flowers, delicious meals with fine wines, fresh food, and desserts. We take vacations during the day. When it comes to *joie de vivre,* neither of us holds anything back.

Is this how you want to live the rest of your life?

She would like an immediate and absolute commitment. But I'm not sure. I'd like more time before committing myself again. I would like to grow more slowly, working problems out as they arise. As for the day-to-day romance, yes, I can handle being happy.

Do you feel that you have lost anything as a result of the affairs that have blown through your life?

Perhaps my sanity at times, but I wouldn't have *not* had any of these experiences. It meant a lot to me when they were happening, and they meant a lot to me afterwards. To this day, I still have beautiful feelings about my time with Emily. Without that, life would be so dull.

For Ilse, there is some regret. We *did* grow up together; we spent half our lifetimes together. I wonder what it would have been like if we had never had kids. Things would have turned out differently with Emily if I hadn't been married with children. Had I known that my relationship with Ilse was going to dead-end the way it did, I would have ended it sooner. Emily and I might have had the chance to share a life together.

What have you gained as a result of your affairs?

Greater dimension—in myself. Affairs aren't just about sex and romance, they're affairs of intimate friendship, mutual growth, and deep connection. When someone else is deeply involved with your inner workings, they are changing and altering you, exposing you to yourself on your deepest levels. You get some pretty heavy messages. You learn them, and keep them, and walk with them the rest of your life. All the feelings I have ever had for Ilse, for Emily, for any woman I have ever loved are all still with me.

The negative side in having an affair is that it's a stolen moment; on the positive side, it is a catalyst for intense personal growth.

How do you see yourself in the future? Do you think you will find one partner who will understand you to the core of your being, whom you can share everything in your life with?

I don't expect it, and I don't look for it. What is more important is to feel the moment and to stay on my own path. Adept women know that the most intense lure to a man is a woman who is clearly on her own path, who is independent and secure, and who possesses her own personality. That kind of self-confidence is undeniably attractive.

The times when relationships are most alive are when both people know that it probably won't last. So if both people live right here, right now, they can find greater meaning in the present. Ask yourself: "If you had only one day to live your life, what would you do?" If each day were lived out that way with someone you love, then it can be the basis for an exquisite and passionate life.

It's easy for people to get so busy and involved with some particular path that they don't have time to enjoy the sunshine. I want to make sure I have time to stop, breathe, and enjoy every moment of my life.

What do you think about the element of secrecy and deceit that seems to be necessary when a married person is having an affair?

There are two problems. The first is how *you* deal with it. Internally, you have to decide how you are going to deal with the situation if you're going to stay married. Whose problem is it really? Is it yours or someone else's?

The second issue is an external one, how *other* people are going to deal with it. You have to decide if you really care what others think. I didn't. I wanted to be open and honest about what was going on. Sometimes that's challenging. I wanted to be able to go to a concert with my lover and be openly affectionate. Even though there were people at the concert who knew I was married to someone else, it was important to me to be really honest about who I was. It would be hypocritical for me to be any other way. I do not want to judge others, nor do I wish to be judged. I want to be part of a changing society whose goals are based on positive values, and I do not want to live in denial. You don't have to flaunt your relationship with your lover, but you don't have to repress it either.

In your opinion, does an open marriage work?

That's like asking if marriage works. The question is not, "Does this work in your life?" The question is, "What do you want in your life?" How do you want to feel? Do you want to be loved? Do you want to be confined by bankrupt societal limits and vacant ethics left over from a code of morality that has outlived its purpose? You can live very safely in complete denial. Yet there's a lot of risk involved in living freely.

There is so much hypocrisy and deception going on in our society right now, ultimately you have to find your own truth and then have the courage to live it. There's a lot of risk in being fully alive—it's complicated and unpredictable, but when your security and predictability is internal, it doesn't matter what strange place or strange situation you are in. The only place you are really going to find your truth is within yourself.

Whatever type of person you think you are doesn't exist: the type to be a wife or husband, the type to be a mother or father, the type to have an affair, whatever. The only type you can be is the type that you are. If you are true to yourself, then you can tell your kids, your spouse, your lover, "This is who I am, and if I am true to myself, then this is the person you love." Remarkably, you don't need to be afraid of losing the people who love you. You do not have to be alone in order to be yourself.

Loving Other People

Julia and Morgan discovered that they wanted to expand their marriage to include others. After some trial and error, they found a way to do this without lying to each other and threatening the love between them.

Julia and Morgan

As a couple, how can you be open to loving other people outside the boundaries of marriage?

Morgan: We love other people *inside* the boundaries of our marriage. It just depends on how you define your marriage.

Julia: When I first got together with Morgan, he was very honest. He said that he wanted to be able to have other lovers, and that he didn't want to lie to me about it. I was relieved when I found out that he didn't want to lie. I hated the thought of being deceived, but it was annoying to be privy to every thought that went through his head, especially thoughts about other women.

I was willing to consider having other lovers, but truthfully, it scared me. It reminded me of the sixties. I remembered being in love with Alan when we both decided to have other lovers. At first, it was great, but eventually, it got out of control. It didn't work because we weren't in touch with our feelings. Nobody admitted to feeling lonely, rejected, hurt, or angry. We thought that highly evolved beings such as ourselves were beyond negative emotions like jealousy or possessiveness.

Alan usually didn't mind my having other relationships, but there were a few times when he did feel threatened. Once, I had an affair with his best friend, which was okay until it became obvious to Alan that his friend wanted me all to himself. I was blind to that fact, and I ignored Alan's feelings. Eventually, I left Alan for his friend, and that was sad because Alan was the father of my child and I did love him. After a while, everything fell apart, including my relationship.

I didn't want that to happen again. So I denied my attraction to other men. I felt uncomfortable when men flirted with me. I covered up my natural beauty by putting on weight; it made me feel safer. And I guarded my relationships by being jealous and possessive, thinking this was the way to prevent disaster from occurring again.

But Morgan challenged me. I like men who dare to be different. After a while, I realized that I was feeling resentful about Morgan's desire for other women, partly because I was suppressing my desire for other men. I wanted to be affectionate with other men, but I wanted the security of a monogamous relationship, too. The first step was for me to recognize that I wasn't being completely truthful with myself.

Is it different for men to have affairs than women?

Julia: In the beginning, Morgan thought he should be able to have affairs, but it would be better if I didn't. He said that women tend to become emotionally attached to their lovers, but that men can have lovers without attachment.

There may be some truth to that, but there were a few flaws in his reasoning. First, whom do men have affairs with? Women! (Usually.) So it was okay for him to have affairs with women who would naturally get attached to him, but he wasn't going to get attached to them? That didn't sound very satisfying for them, and it *did* sound threatening to me.

Can affairs and marriages co-exist?

Morgan: I want to define an "affair." An affair is something that takes place outside marriage. It usually happens because the two people in the marriage aren't growing together, or they are in a relationship they don't want to be in, but they don't want to give up the security. So one partner or the other finds someone else to fulfill what's missing. They are trying to patch it from the outside.

When I am feeling really full and loving within myself, I am able to love every woman who comes along, I see the goddess in every woman. But when I am not feeling good about my wife, no other woman is going to substitute for her. This is a very secure relationship because we both know that neither of us is going anywhere; there's no point in starting over with anyone else. However, it's not possible for one person to be everything at all times for another person. Monogamy is an illusion. It doesn't exist. I don't think that there is one monogamous relationship in the kind of open society that we have. People may pretend to be monogamous, and they may not actually have "in and out" sex with another partner, but they are always looking around and fantasizing.

Maybe men do it more overtly than women. Women are a little more secretive about it; they do it more subtly, but they love to watch men. So I really don't think there is any such thing as monogamy; all we have is "pretend" monogamy.

How have you been able to create an "open marriage"?

Morgan: I don't like to use the term "open marriage." For one thing, that implies that all other marriages are closed, which is probably true. But when most people refer to an open marriage, it implies that each partner goes in his or her own direction. With us there is a very strong commitment to each other. We share whatever is happening to either of us, both as a couple and as individuals. I don't think that we could do what we do without that strong bond between us.

Although I love Julia and I am married to her, I don't own her and I have no right to control her. Whether she is going to stay with me or leave me depends on who I am and what I am doing, and on who she is and what she is doing. That is what I have learned to accept.

To be able to love powerfully and deeply is to be able to love generously. It is the outgrowth of the love that we have for each other that we are able to share with others. When we're not getting along, or when either one of us is uncomfortable with a situation, it doesn't feel like a desirable option to be sexual with someone else. Then it feels as if one of us is going outside the marriage. But when we are feeling good together, it feels natural to bring others into that overflow of love.

Do either of you still feel threatened when your partner is enjoying the company of someone of the opposite sex?

Julia: At first, I was infuriated when Morgan suggested that I choose another woman for him. He said that he wanted me to choose someone I liked before he got interested in someone I didn't like. But after we had been together for over a year, I was convinced that he loved me and didn't want to hurt me. We set up a set of boundaries that felt good to both of us. We agreed to always put each other first, and not to let anyone else come between us. We also agreed that we would try not to get involved with anyone whom the other person didn't like. Our understanding is that we will both be open with each other about what we really feel, and when feelings do arise, we will try and deal with them right away. That creates a climate of safety and security.

Morgan: *Try* is the key word here. Whenever we make an agreement, it is an intention rather than a rule. We both acknowledge that unpredictable things can happen, and we don't always have complete control over our emotions. We have found that if we ignore our feelings, and sweep them under the carpet, sooner or later we will trip over them. So we are constantly learning to communicate with each other.

Did either of you ever have a secret affair?

Julia: When I was single, I fell in love with a married man, Walter. It was very painful for me because his wife Mona was my friend. She knew that Walter and I were good friends, and she trusted me. Since they both confided in me, I knew that they hadn't been sexual with each other for over a year. They were miserable and both of them wanted a separation. The only reason they stayed together was because they had young children.

I had no intention of falling in love with Walter. But our friendship got closer and deeper until one day he asked me to have an affair with him. By that time, I desperately wanted to hold him in my arms and make love with him. It would have been fine if we could have told Mona, but since she was Catholic, he was sure she could never accept it.

I was convinced that if Walter and I became lovers, it would have been easier for him to endure the marriage until the kids grew up, but I didn't want to take him away from her. Walter and I wanted each other very much, but I couldn't handle the deception. If we became lovers, it would drive me crazy, and it would have ruined my reputation in the community. It would also have destroyed my friendship with Mona. On the other hand, if Mona had been willing to let Walter have an affair, I would have gladly accepted the challenge of trying to work it out with them.

While I was struggling with this moral dilemma, I confided in several different friends. One woman was shocked that I would even consider such a thing, but the others said, in effect, to go for it. During that period, I was amazed by all the stories of secret affairs my friends were having.

Walter and I never became lovers, and I am so glad that we never opened Pandora's Box. To me, that box symbolizes the insanity that ensues when you mix powerful emotions of love and affection with deception and guilt. Eventually, I moved away. Walter continued to call me every week for a year. Then he left his wife, and we arranged a rendezvous and made passionate love for three days and nights. It was marvelous. After that, he didn't call. Three weeks later, I was going crazy and made some pretext to call his wife. She told me that he came back because he missed the kids so much. I thought to myself, "If someone had told me a year ago that I could have saved Walter's marriage a year ago by making love to him, I would have gladly done it." By this time, I was really in love with him, and it ripped me apart. But I just told myself, "Give thanks for what you have had, and let the rest go." So I did.

What about you, Morgan?

Morgan: When I was single, I almost had an affair with a married woman. I met Joel when he hired me to build a greenhouse on his property. I was out there working my tail off eight hours a day, and his wife, Samantha, would bring me cold drinks. I had absolutely no interest in her. She was not my type, and she had two sweet little kids. Besides, she was married to Joel, and I liked him. But we got to talking, and she seemed really desperate to find someone who would listen to her. She loved it when I paid attention to her kids. Then one day, she came over to my house because she had a gift for me. That really surprised me. By that time, Joel was beginning to notice, and he was getting uptight. When she was over at my house, she confessed that she was in love with me. I didn't want to get involved, even though I liked her and I was really horny. When she assured me that her marriage was on the rocks, I said, "You need to resolve whatever is going on between the two of you, and then we will see what's happening with us."

A while later, she called to tell me that she'd left her husband and was staying at a cabin in the woods. She asked me if I would join her. We finally became lovers. About a month after that, her husband moved out of the house, and she persuaded me to move in with her.

Usually people have difficulty integrating a love affair and a marriage, and can rarely be whole in either one. How have the two of you dealt with this?

Morgan: It has been only within the last hundred years that people have attempted to put love and marriage together in one package. We have a myth that love and marriage go together and last forever, and it's just not true.

People have also bought into the concept of scarcity, so that monogamy as it is conventionally practiced nurtures the idea that there's not enough to go around.

Now that we are faced with trying to fulfill all our needs *inside* the boundaries of marriage, we don't have any operational guidelines. So we experiment by trial and error as we go along.

When was the first time you, as a couple, successfully experimented with your new approach to love and marriage?

Julia: One night at a party, I met a woman, Laura, whom I really liked. I was attracted to her, and I could feel that she was attracted to me. It felt sensual and delicious between us, and I thought it would be perfect if Morgan liked her too. Later that evening, I saw Laura with Morgan, and I was pleased. After a while, he came up and introduced her to me, not knowing we had already met. Morgan and I both grinned when Laura realized that I was Morgan's wife.

Later, she came to our house, and we all cuddled together. We didn't actually make love, but we did enjoy each other. Morgan could be affectionate with her, and she could be affectionate with me, and the circle was complete. It wasn't a loss for me; it was a gain.

I could really feel Morgan's love for me when we were all together. He didn't want to push me away; he wanted to include me. Like most men, he was turned on by the idea of making love to two women. Ordinarily, that wouldn't have been very exciting for me, except that I found out how delightful it was to be sensual with another woman. Morgan loved to watch us loving each other.

Then came the bonus. Laura said she wanted us to meet her boyfriend, Ron. She admitted that she liked Morgan because he and Ron were so much alike. She explained that Ron and she had an open relationship, and we agreed to get together. The following week, we all went out to dinner together. Ron and I were immediately attracted to each other. Ron and Morgan liked each other too. The four of us felt totally at home with one another. That was almost a year ago. We have been enjoying each other's company ever since.

Has any doubt, jealousy, or competition arisen during the course of this relationship?

Julia: Those emotions come up sometimes—especially in the beginning when Ron and I were having such a marvelous time together, but Laura handled it beautifully. She didn't try to control him out of fear or insecurity, and she didn't try to stop us from being together. She just asked us to stay with her until she could feel loved by all of us. She knew how to ask for what she needed, and we all loved her enough to want to give it to her. We love and trust each other enough to share our men.

Morgan, how have you dealt with jealousy in Julia?

Morgan: Julia hasn't been jealous of Laura, because she gets as much out of being with her as I do. The only problem I had was when I got interested in Sandra, a woman she didn't trust. At first, Julia ranted and raved, and then she withdrew. I realized that I was overreacting because she reminded me of my mother. I had shut down just to protect myself. Then I wanted to try and help Julia, to make her feel better, but she didn't want to be fixed. From her point of view, there was nothing wrong with her. She just wanted to let off steam.

Now, if she gets jealous, we lie on the bed together and I hold her. I reassure her and I let her talk. I don't try to defend myself, and I don't make her feel wrong for feeling as she does. When she gets that reassurance, she usually feels better. But I have learned that it doesn't work for me to be with someone she doesn't feel safe with.

Julia: After the situation with Sandra, I realized that Morgan is not responsible for what I feel. I am in charge of what I feel. I can't blame him for making me feel a certain way. However, he needs to know that if he chooses to be with someone I don't like, I am probably going to feel crazy.

The key element to your success seems to be that you know that even if Morgan is loving another women, he never stops loving you. Does that enhance your ability to love him?

Julia: Yes. The unique thing about Morgan is the extent to which he has demonstrated how much he cares about me. In subtle little ways, even if he is with another woman, he continues to let me know that he is still with me and loves me. But the first time I was openly affectionate with another man, we were at a party and I didn't do for Morgan all those subtle little things that he does for me—keeping eye contact, checking in with him, reminding me that he loves me. I didn't do any of that, and it hurt him.

Afterward he asked, "If I had done that to you, how would you have felt?" Then I saw that I was doing to him what I had always been afraid that he would do to me. I realized that my biggest fear had been that he would go off with someone else and not love me.

But that isn't what he wants. Even if he's with someone else, I can always go to him and not feel that I am interrupting something. If I am feeling insecure, I know that they will comfort me. That's why it's so important that we both feel good about who the other person is with. It makes us feel that we are welcome in each other's lives.

How do you deal with the issue of sexually transmitted disease?

Julia: For all our talk, we have been intimately involved with only one other couple, Ron and Laura, who are very conscientious people. When the four of us decided to become lovers, we had a "safe sex" talk. We shared sexual histories and made sure that AIDS tests had been taken. Beyond that, our understanding is that if we make love with other people, it will be protected sex.

Are Ron and Laura still a vital part of your life?

Julia: Yes. When we don't see each other for a while, I miss her as much as I miss him. When we come back from being with Ron and Laura, we come home much happier and more appreciative of each other. I am glad I am able to express myself in this way.

Morgan: We don't see them as often as we'd like, but we call each other. There's been one surprising benefit to our relationship with them. When Julia and I come to an impasse on something, we can call on them for help. When there's another couple in your life, there are two other viewpoints on any given issue. Sometimes it feels as though all three people are ganging up on you, but it's really hard to argue with three people so I have to consider that maybe they're right. It's a whole different dynamic in a relationship; it's hard to get stuck in a battle of wills.

Julia: I feel one hundred percent better about this marriage than any other marriage I've been involved in. In the past, marriage for me was static and uncreative. It was a ball and chain, even if I was with someone I really loved. With Morgan, it just gets better and better; it's ever expanding. The love and tenderness between us gets richer and richer. We're in the process of getting to know each other, instead of trying to make each other into what we want the other person to be.

I feel incredibly blessed. It's rare to have one really good relationship, but to have three loving partners is almost unbelievable.

Morgan: For me it is the fulfillment of the kind of relationship I have always wanted—a solid, committed, and loving marriage with the possibility of expanding that circle of love. In many ways, it's a dream come true.

Love without Expectations

As a man who teaches about the healing power of love, Justin practices what he preaches. A man who lives in the present, he finds it easy to love many women, yet he is completely available to whomever he is in a relationship with at any given moment. Out of his own beliefs, Justin truly embraces everyone he meets with all of his being.

Justin

Do you consider yourself monogamous?

There are times in my life when I have wanted to be with one only person. Some people would call that "faithful," but I don't since it just happens to be what I wanted to do at the time. For the majority of my life, I haven't felt as though I wanted to be monogamous. In some cases, I found myself *trying* to be monogamous, which just ruined the sensuous and spontaneous aspects of the relationship. So I decided to stop trying, to let myself be and do what I wanted to do. So now, when I decide to take a walk with a beautiful woman or hold someone in my arms for a while, I am not cheating on anybody.

We tend to think of monogamy as a sexual thing, but true monogamy is to have that state of consciousness in which you are not interested in anyone else. With that definition, I don't think anybody is really monogamous.

I don't think there is anything wrong with appreciating a beautiful woman and wanting to know how she feels. Is that breaking a monogamous bond with your wife? Some people would say yes, and some people would say no.

Do you think that it's healthy to be attracted to other people?

I think that the capacity to love more than one person, to be with more than one person is a natural thing. To deny this expression is to cause imbalance.

Do you think that traditional monogamy revolves around issues of ownership, control, security, fear, and jealousy? Are these the demons that fly out of Pandora's Box?

That's all they are.

How does a person contain that natural curiosity to love someone else within the boundaries prescribed by our social order? Is that why people lie?

It's all a matter of not being true to yourself. That's the source of all disease, all suffering, all pain.

What is the answer to that—not to marry?
The institution of marriage, as we understand it, is built upon fear—the fear of losing security and control over each other. But that is not to say that a one-on-one relationship has no value. I have had several long-term relationships, living with one woman for years at a time, and I found that very fulfilling.

A marriage certificate can be like a contract for monogamy; it creates an artificial boundary that can always be broken. In some cases, there is the fear that one partner really would rather be with someone else.

A healthy relationship thrives on an innate loyalty and sense of acceptance. There is permission to explore feelings with others, with an understanding that the partner will always come home. That takes a tremendous amount of acceptance, appreciation, and love. There is greater love in that kind of freedom, the freedom to live spontaneously from the heart and in the moment. Both appreciation and curiosity are a normal part of life.

In light of all this, do you think that having an affair is immoral?
Not at all.

Why do you think that affairs are considered immoral?
It is society's attempt to control our behavior. Affairs take place underground; they are revolutionary. It's part of our dark side that we think we have to get rid of. By its nature, society wants to expose what's hidden and secret.

What's been instrumental in my life, for maintaining my personal freedom, is having an inner space that no one knows about. My relationship with you has nothing to do with anyone else in the world; it's just between you and me.

Our society promotes what I call a "spill-the-beans" consciousness where as a good wife you are supposed to tell your husband absolutely everything that you did all day. That's not real intimacy. Most people don't know what intimacy is. They think it just means confessing everything. To me, living with intimacy means accepting and appreciating another human being beyond expectations, conditions, and need.

Do you think that secrecy gives an affair its destructive power?
Society just judges it and punishes the "guilty." Anything or anyone that threatens to break its boundaries must be punished and controlled.

Don't you think that it's a high price to pay—to lose a marriage, a career, or social status in the community?

It's ridiculous. The repercussions can be devastating. People don't know what to do once the energy starts moving.

What is this energy?

It's in everyone, the part of you that loves to be touched, held, loved, and cuddled in a physical way. It seems that we have to justify touching someone. Just touching someone because you want to isn't okay. We need to have reasons for everything we want to do.

I meet so many women who are frustrated with what's going on in their personal and professional lives. At least eighty percent of the women I meet in my work are either single or divorced, or would like to be divorced. There doesn't seem to be much room for marriage and intimacy.

Do you come across many people who are totally happy with what they are doing?

No. Most of the women I talk to feel that they are baby-sitting their men. That's what they say to me. Then they go through the same cycle of marrying the same man again in various different forms.

Why do you think these women keep resorting to marriage? If that form of relationship isn't working, why do they keep doing it?

Because they lack the courage to be okay with themselves without the security of marriage. When a woman is truly secure within herself, she doesn't care about the piece of paper—the marriage contract.

The body is for experiencing the senses of life—feeling the sun and water, feeling the passion of lovemaking. There's nothing dirty about it; it's the most wonderful thing there is.

Why do you think people have such a hard time giving themselves permission to feel this?

Guilt. If it's outside marriage, they don't want to go beyond the boundaries of what they feel they are allowed to do. Even women who are single and available often have a wall up beyond which they just can't let go. When they finally do, they sob and cry and don't know what to do with this freedom and power.

Would you define your role as that of a sex therapist?

You could say that. Over the past ten years, I have met so many women who are unhappy in marriage and want to get divorced. It's the classic scenario. Perhaps they are sheltered, uneducated, and inexperienced in life.

One of these women became my secretary. She married at seventeen, had children, and never had another boyfriend in her life. She had never even had a job before. She was beautiful and intelligent but had not experienced much of life. We had an affair, and it triggered a whole new dimension in her life. She wanted to get a divorce instantly, and she did.

That scenario has happened repeatedly in my life. Fortunately, most of the women I have had these relationships with are still my friends, although we may no longer have a sexual relationship. But sometimes it backfires and can destroy a person's life. I think that comes from not knowing how to channel the energy once it is released. It has to keep moving forward; there's no going back once the energy has broken loose. You can't stop the wave or you'll drown. You just have to ride the surf, and not think about it too much, or you'll miss it. You just have to go with the flow and have courage.

How have you dealt with the phenomenon of jealousy—the jealous husband or jealous boyfriend?

I have dealt with a lot of jealous women, but not many jealous men. I am usually very direct. I am not trying to steal anyone away from anyone else. A woman is a free human being; she has the right to do whatever she chooses. Nobody owns anyone else, and I am very clear about that. If a jealous man wants to get into a fight, I am willing to do that, too, and I will protect myself so that I don't get hurt.

How do you deal with the inevitable attachments that arise in these women whom you have "set free?" Isn't it natural that they would develop a new attachment to you once they've left their marriage?

That's been really difficult, especially since my life involves so much traveling. It doesn't work for me to have anyone traveling with me. I don't want to have to take someone else's needs into consideration. I have to be available and accommodating to the people I am teaching, and I don't want to have to do that twenty-four hours a day. I need to spend a certain amount of time alone.

I feel guilty that I don't spend more time near my daughter, but I have to be true to myself, and ultimately the only gift I can give my daughter is the example of living true to my own passion.

Once, I was engaged to be married. I would have been very happily married, but my fiancée left me for another woman. I cried and got upset for about five minutes, but after that I couldn't get angry. What I found is that I really loved her, and whatever she wanted to do was okay. In many ways, she did me a tremendous favor. She set me on my current path which took me in a completely different direction.

In general, what do you think of people who have affairs?

I think they owe it to themselves to do what they want to do. If you don't do what you really want to do in your life, you're only fooling yourself. Having an affair doesn't mean that you're going to end your marriage. Life is supposed to be about doing what you want to do, whether you are married or single.

It's odd, because I haven't used the word "affair" for about five or six years, but I guess in the eyes of society, that's what I am doing—having a series of affairs. Maybe it's because I am not married, nor have I chosen one person to be with. When we're younger, we just call it dating different people. When we get older we call it having affairs. It's all a matter of semantics. An "affair" is a very connotative word. It's hard to use it without implying a sense of betrayal.

Some people believe that having an affair can be a healthy thing, it can revive a relationship that has gotten stuck in its patterns, or it can fulfill one partner whose needs haven't been met. Often loving a new person can open the door and let the light in. An affair can rekindle some joy, spontaneity, and passion in life. And often, there's more energy to take home to the other partner, if he or she can be open enough to accept it. Do you think that such a scenario is possible?

I was once living with a woman who went away on a vacation for a few weeks. She hadn't been very happy before she left, and when she got back, I could tell immediately that she had an affair while she was gone. She felt really guilty and didn't want to talk about it. I decided to wait for her to deal with it in her own way. Instead of confronting her about it, I just held her and loved her. After a while, it melted away and she never really had to talk about it. To me, it just enhanced who she was. When she finally told me about it a year or so later, she said that having the affair had really sharpened her appreciation for me; it made her realize that I was the one she wanted to be with. Really loving her meant that I didn't want to make her feel bad for what had happened. It was just an experience that she wanted to have.

It's not even a matter of forgiveness. That's a word I have tried to throw out of my vocabulary. Forgiveness implies that one person has power over another and is somehow morally better than the other; it implies that someone did something wrong.

The classical reaction when someone finds out that his or her partner is having an affair is to take a very self-righteous stance: indignation, rejection, anger. The person who had the affair asks the other person for forgiveness. The "wronged" person holds the power and decides whether or not to grant a pardon. Sometimes an affair is the catalyst for greater healing and intimacy between a couple. Other times, the "wronged" one chooses to hang onto the anger and pain, which only serves to end the relationship.

It all comes down to forgiveness, which often reduces the "unfaithful" one to the status of a whimpering puppy. Don't you think that it creates more anger, resentment, and humiliation—especially if the person who had the affair doesn't feel that there was anything wrong in what he or she did?

Rather than forgiving someone, it is sometimes healthier just to accept it, let go, and appreciate what's happening. It's difficult, but that way you can avoid the chain reaction of guilt-based emotion. Focus on what I call the three A's: acceptance, appreciation, and awareness. Awareness is the result of acceptance and appreciation.

How do these affairs happen in your life?

Somehow the appreciation I have gained for myself spills over. Just because I like myself, and enjoy my life, women seem to want to be around me. There are so many women who are unhappy in their lives, they want to talk and have tea, they want someone to listen to. One thing leads to another, and you wake up in bed with them the next morning.

Is that satisfying to you?

I would never be with someone unless I really wanted to be with that person. Years ago, when I was studying tantra, I learned how to do all kinds of things with my body sexually, but I found that kind of performance sex to be very empty. Even if I am with a gorgeous woman who wants to sleep with me, my body will be completely impotent no matter what is done. It used to bother me, but now I find it interesting just to watch what happens.

The physical act of union is just one part of the whole experience of lovemaking, which to me involves tenderness, expressing feelings, cuddling, being playful, making tea for each other—all that stuff. Everything a couple does together is lovemaking. Lovers bring out different harmonics in each other.

Sometimes there are women who are looking for a quick fix; they don't know anything else is out there. They're just looking for a fling so that they can stay in the safety of their marriage and career and be taken care of.

For a while, I felt that I was being used. It made me feel cheap. So I stopped having those kinds of relationships because I felt I wasn't being appreciated.

As a metaphysical teacher, you must meet a lot of people who come to you with their problems, expect you to have all the answers and to make their lives better. That's a lot to expect from another human being. How do you deal with that?

When I don't meet people's expectations, they can get very angry. It's very difficult when I am giving a talk. Sometimes women in the room get jealous of each other over me, and none of them has even talked to me!

At times I feel like a metaphysical rock-and-roll star. It's absurd. I like the attention, but I don't like the calamities that can result. It can get ridiculous. I don't like to be worshiped. I'm not some guru that comes to bless his followers and then disappears in a cloud of mystery. I like being an ordinary person, and I like to be with people. I'm just here. When there's no mystery, there's no worship.

How do you deal with jealousy in women?

Jealous women are hard to deal with. Men are very direct; you can go outside and punch it out. But that doesn't work with women. I just have to dance with all of it. I love to be around women, but I can't handle being with a woman who is trying to change me or control me with her jealousy. I just have to be who I am. It's all part of loving someone; if you love someone, you don't want to control him or her because that is just putting conditions on that person's behavior. What I am finding now is that women who are attracted to me seem to understand this, and jealousy isn't so much of a problem. They just back out of a competitive scene.

Who is the perfect woman for you?

Part of me would like to have one partner to be with and share it all, but it would have to be someone who doesn't "need" me and won't cling to me. She would have to have her own life. We would walk parallel paths, but be traveling in the same direction with the same destination.

So do you have room in your life for one special partner?

Definitely. But I am not interested in shopping. I am steering away from new age one-night stands, and people who send marriage proposals through the mail. I am finding I enjoy women who like to take care of me, not those who just want to see what they can get out of me. It's a whole different energy. It fills me up rather than drains me.

It's amazing to be with a woman who simply wants to love me, someone who doesn't want anything at all from me, someone who just enjoys being with me.

Have you ever had affair while you were living with someone else?

Only once, and it drew that relationship to a very quick conclusion. Usually if I am living with someone, it's because I want to be with that person, and no one else. There was one really special woman. Even when I was seeing another woman, it made me realize how special she was to me. It made me want to be with her more. So I stopped the affair and became even more dedicated to our relationship.

Love never really ends; it just changes its form. We're not living together anymore, but we are still an integral part of each other's worlds. We still love each other. She doesn't really care if she's with someone or not. That's what I like about her. She feels whole within herself whether she is with a man or not.

So many women do not feel whole unless they are with a man and will tolerate incredible abuse just for that security. Then if they fail in such a relationship, they think there is something wrong with them. Would you say that this is why you meet so many unhappy women?

Yes, and when they get a taste of freedom, they get intoxicated. If they have an affair, they will expect more from the affair than it can honestly give them. So often these affairs are really just springboards to release the energy that has been all locked up.

It doesn't really matter who has the key that unlocks the door. That's why it is so important for people who get involved in affairs not to hold expectations about what the affairs are supposed to be.

Just be with the moment—love and appreciate what's going on. Maybe you'll be together for a hundred years, maybe you won't. It doesn't matter. What matters is the love and caring that you experience together when you are together.

How does an affair usually end for you?

Usually because I travel a lot, it just changes form. The good feelings continue, though. I'm not interested in busting up marriages. I just check in as any good friend would.

If the affair involves more than just a sexual attraction, and you really love each other it doesn't matter if you are in one another's presence or not. Communication is what's really important.

Didn't you go through a phase of your life when you were celibate?

For three years, between the ages of nineteen and twenty-two. I chose that time period because I had become really adept at different psychic phenomena, and I didn't want to distract myself with sex. It was strange at first, but I noticed that whenever you drop something out of your life, something else always takes its place. I was very fulfilled by doing what I was doing. Celibacy is like monogamy. It's something that has to occur naturally, or it's not really genuine.

What are your feelings for the women you have had affairs with?

There isn't anyone I've been with that I don't have a really strong love for and care for deeply. When I see them again, there's a lot of joy and affection. In any relationship that I've ever had, there's never been any bitterness that lasted any longer than about five minutes. Many of my lovers look back on our time together and feel a special connection with me, no matter what else may take place in their lives.

What have you gained from these experiences?
I get to see over and over again that I really do live the principles that I teach other people—to love simply, without expectations and conditions. I have learned to be content with who I am, and I do not really need anyone else. I just love other people for who they are and appreciate them completely. The love between us comes and goes like waves of energy.

I am completely involved one hundred percent with what I am doing and whom I am with, in the present. I am not daydreaming about someone else. I try not to let love possess me.

The teachings I share are extremely intimate, and sometimes I have to be able to share that intimacy with five hundred people in one room so that each person experiences it personally.

Have you lost anything as a result of these experiences?
Society promotes the image of the wife and the family and the house with the white picket fence. There are times when I am traveling alone that I question what I am doing, but those feelings don't stay for long, because I remember the pain that those attachments can bring. It takes a lot of courage to let things go their natural way.

What is your advice to people who are tortured by having an affair, people who see it as a crisis that threatens to destroy their life as they have always known it?
Don't hold onto your life as you have always known it. Let it be what it is now. Then you will realize that it is okay. Letting your life change is okay. Perhaps your fear arises from living by other people's standards.

Make your decisions. Live in your decisions. Accept what you are doing. Love and appreciate what you have chosen in your life. Ultimately, no one judges you but yourself. Worrying about what other people think of you, worrying about ruining your reputation, all those things are the classic demons that come out of Pandora's Box.

Pandora's Box is nothing more than society's concepts, structures, beliefs, and traditions, and each of us judges ourselves according to how our behavior conforms or does not conform. It's really nobody's business what you do. You don't have to confess anything to your partner, to your boss, to your hairdresser, and certainly not to your psychologist.

What do you think of someone who has an affair just to get even with somebody?

Having an affair out of revenge or spite is silly. Do things because you want to do them, not because you want to hurt someone. Having an affair just to get even usually backfires.

What do you say to people who keep the existence of an affair a deep, dark secret that slowly erodes their souls?

It's not important whether or not you tell anybody about your secret. What's important is to let go within yourself so that you feel okay about it. It's not healthy to hold on to a secret, any secret, and strangle yourself with it. If something is haunting you, let it go, realizing that you haven't done anything bad. There is no judgment in life other than self-judgment. Having an affair, having an abortion, getting a divorce—it's all okay. It's all a matter of learning to flow with the natural changes of life.

Betrayed by Destiny

Estelle's affair with Charles went on for years, while she waited patiently for him to tell his wife that he wanted to end their marriage. He finally confronted his wife with the truth in a counseling session and afterward went out sailing alone, something he always loved to do.

He was following his usual course across the bay when a surprise squall blew in from out of the south. As the storm's intensity built, he lost his tiller and drowned. Devastated, Estelle felt betrayed by destiny. She is now rebuilding her life one day at a time.

Estelle

Had you ever had an affair before you met Charles?

About ten years ago, I was in a committed relationship with Frank. While I was with him, I had an affair that I couldn't tell him about. I felt so terrible that I ended the relationship with Frank without telling him why. I was punishing myself. The affair went against everything I knew about myself, and I couldn't understand why I had let it happen.

Several months later, we dated again in an attempt to reconstruct our relationship. Out of a desire to clear up the past, I told him about the affair. Telling the truth was a mistake. He kicked me out of his house and didn't talk to me for six months.

So I was without a man for the first time in my life. I had to face myself and what I had done. That's when I realized that I had consistently chosen to be with men who were critical and abusive—who were devastating to my self-esteem. I realized that I had suffered incest as a child but hadn't told Frank about it. I hadn't even dealt with it myself. I saw that I was sabotaging any chance for love in my life.

As my own awareness began to awaken, I knew I had to stand my ground and say no to the abuse. It was crazy being in these psychotic dead-end relationships. I realized that I needed *not* to be in a relationship with anybody for a while, so that I could make some sense out of my life. I started reading a lot of self-help books, and I cried a lot.

How did you deal with your daughter at this time?

It was rough. It was hard to overcome the darkness that seemed to overshadow our lives. I was floundering emotionally, but I couldn't cry in front of Jenny. I had to be the strong one. One night I remember sitting out by the cliffs, shivering in the night, tears streaming down my face so that I could cry alone. I wanted permission from the universe to be human and cry.

That's when Charles came into my life. The first time I fell in love with him, my boyfriend and I were at the beach. I had met Charles a few times socially, so I recognized him as he walked along the beach with his son, Jeff, who is autistic. I cried as I watched his kindness with Jeff. Charles was so patient in dealing with Jeff's frustration and fears. I instantly loved Charles for his devotion and commitment to that child. I ran into him again at parties. We had a lot of mutual friends. I noticed that when he was with his wife, Elizabeth, he was very distant. They would be awkward and uptight, hanging out on the sidelines instead of mingling. But when it was time to dance, he would cut loose like a wild man.

Sometimes I would see him when I went out sailing with a group of friends. One time he called and asked me to go sailing with him alone. I refused several times, and then he confronted me by saying, "I know you are saying no because of Elizabeth." One time we had been at a party and I was dancing. I could feel the penetrating intensity of his gaze; I looked and our eyes met. Elizabeth saw it too and has hated me ever since. Even after I expressed my fear of her jealousy, he said, "I know, but I feel so isolated. I need you as my friend." He hoped that she would get over her jealousy. So I agreed to go sailing with him, and it was great.

Later he asked me to go dancing. Elizabeth was off doing something, so it was just the two of us. We had a fun, light evening. There were lots of beautiful women where we were dancing. When I commented on that, he leaned over and said, "I would trade all of them for just one of you." After that, I got scared. I asked him to drive me home. Before saying good night, I said, "If we are going to be friends, we have to create an environment which is safe." Then he made another pass at me, and I got out of the car as fast as I could.

The next time we went for a bike ride with several mutual friends. He pretended as though nothing had happened. But he began stopping by my house on the spur of the moment, and spent time getting to know my daughter. We would even share moments of silence together—a comfortable, beautiful silence.

He went on a vacation to Mexico with his wife and came back very distraught because she wouldn't even go to the beach with him. He was sad that they didn't know how to have fun together.

Did it feel as though you were having an affair?
Not until he called and invited me to go to Hawaii with him on a vacation. I confessed my attraction to him, and admitted that I was having fantasies about him. I asked if he intended to have an affair with me. At first he denied it and said he merely wanted to go surfing and have fun. Finally he admitted

that he had the same feelings, too. I told him, "I do not want to have an affair with a married man, but I love being with you." So he agreed to invite his friend, Jerry, to come along as a chaperone. I agreed.

I was very excited. We always seemed to bring out the adventure and passion in each other. The first night, the three of us went out to dinner, and then we decided to go dancing. I began dancing with Jerry, and then Charles grabbed me on the dance floor; we were swept away by the passion that had been building between us. The people watching us were breathless, and the crowd parted to make way for us in the center of the circle. It was like something out of a movie. The energy between us was so dynamic and alive— something I had never experienced.

Then we went back to the hotel room and tried to sleep, which was of course impossible. Once Jerry was asleep, Charles and I took a bath together and made love passionately all night long. Our affair was consummated at last, and we continued to make love every single night of the entire vacation. Jerry was discreet about it; he was just so delighted to see his friend happy again.

Charles was savage. I guess he was getting in touch with his animal nature. I realized how much sexual energy he had been repressing in his marriage. So, we played savage for the next eight days. We had an understanding that what had happened was just a vacation, and we had to go back to reality. He said that he had no intention of leaving his wife, that our affair had nothing to do with his marriage. It was only about releasing passion. I agreed with him completely.

Was it hard to let go of the affair and pretend it hadn't happened?
On the plane I cried, and then I realized what joy it had brought me to be with him. He had paid for everything, and I felt happier than I had felt for a long time, so I relaxed and accepted it for what it was.

About four days later, there was a knock at my door. It was Charles. He asked to come in and immediately grabbed me the way he had on the dance floor. He said, "I can't stay away from you. I have fallen in love with you. I want to have fun in my life. I got back to Elizabeth and realized that I'm not in love with her, that I've never been in love with her. There's no passion between us. I haven't felt this way for fifteen years." He said that the raw sensuality of making love in the jungle was a welcome contrast to the lacy boudoir he had been used to.

Did you feel the need to make love in a lacy boudoir too?
Yes, occasionally, he would rent a wedding suite at a hotel, with room service and champagne, but we both felt it was wrong. It was a real dilemma for me. One of the things I loved about him was his devotion to his family, and I didn't want to be in the role of the home wrecker.

He was still loving, and nonjudgmental. He listened to all I had to say—about my moral misgivings, my own inability to make a commitment, and my old fear that I didn't deserve to be loved. If there's anything Charles did for me, it was to make me feel that I deserved love in my life.

I respect him for spending so much energy trying to find a way out of his marriage that would not hurt his family. Charles said that he had figured out a way to do it, but that it would take some time. He said, "I know you are the woman I am meant to be with. We will spend the rest of our lives together." I was willing to wait.

I said I would give him a year. The affair began to get really painful, but the secrecy added fire to the passion. Being together was a complete and utter delight, but when it was time for him to leave, I would feel devastated. I was his mistress, and it made me feel very empty. I even had to hide our affair from my daughter.

After a year and a half, I said I couldn't handle it anymore. I needed to start seeing other men. People were beginning to wonder why I wasn't dating anyone. I was feeling tortured. I needed a relationship that I could be open about, I needed to be with someone I could be seen in public with, I needed an honest date.

After that, we kept running into each other in public, and he wouldn't even acknowledge me. It hurt so much. He would say hello, but that was all. He said that if he were seen talking to me, it would cause a scandal. It made me feel as if I didn't exist.

Did you try to end it?

I ended it every month. Then he would call two weeks later. I would resist him, and then I would give in after a week. When he would say, "I appreciate how hard this is for you," I would melt. At one point, we went six months without seeing each other. When we got together again, he said, "I have never lost sight of the fact that we are meant to spend eternity together." Then he would tell me how he and Elizabeth were doing in counseling, and the steps he was taking to end their marriage.

Did you ever think that he was lying to you?

No. He talked about marrying me and wanting me to have his baby. He loved every inch of my body. To him it was sacred.

He loved that I was strong and had raised my daughter alone, that I had a career and still had integrity. He never held back anything. He would say, "You don't know how much I am going to spoil and pamper you when we are finally together. I've never met anyone who deserves it more. I appreciate what you are sacrificing by waiting for me. I'm going to shower you with love and affection." There was no way I could resist the power of that kind of love.

He told me to get my passport, because we were going to go traveling around the world. He was very sure that he could create whatever he wanted. He has always been that way. He recognizes what he wants and makes it happen without any doubt whatsoever. That conviction eliminated a lot of my fear. I trusted him.

What was going on between Charles and Elizabeth in counseling?
He promised me that he would never tell her about his affair with me. We even had a ceremony to consecrate the promise. I knew that it would be so damaging, it would destroy everything. So he went through the counseling with her, acknowledging that he was unhappy and exploring her role in that unhappiness. She tried her hardest to change for him. Even in one-to-one counseling, he could not admit to having an affair. This denial went on for a long time.

When did the truth finally come out?
I stopped seeing Charles and was dating other men. About a year ago, Charles came to me and asked if I had fallen in love with someone else. Even though I was having sex with other men, I knew I was still in love with Charles. So we made love again and I broke it off with the other men the very next day.

Then I realized that I couldn't continue doing that until he cleared things up with Elizabeth. I had to take care of myself. Again he asked me to wait. I told him to do whatever he had to do to end things with her, and then we could be together.

A few months later, he came over with a gift, and said that he was leaving Elizabeth. He had already told her that he had decided to move out. Next, he was going to tell the rest of his family. He told me he had made an agreement with her to remain celibate during their separation. I decided to honor that. Step by step, it was fascinating to watch him execute his plan to extricate himself from his marriage.

What was your relationship like during his separation?
Very interesting. There was an awkwardness between us because of the imposed celibacy. Even when he picked me up for a date, I felt like he was looking at what I had chosen to wear, comparing it to what Elizabeth would have worn. He wouldn't sit close to me, because he was still afraid of being in public with me. I wanted to be free, spontaneous, and uninhibited in expressing my feelings, as I was when I was with Joe, the man I had recently been seeing. I couldn't help but compare them.

But one night, we did go out to dinner and a movie. I paid for everything. Charles finally seemed to be at peace and was very clear about the future.

Afterward, we went out on the cliffs and made love. That was the last time we were together.

Had he made peace with his wife?
They spent that last weekend together, but he was clear with me that he would never be her lover again. He wanted her to know that he loved her, but that he was not in love with her. He wanted her to be with someone who *was* in love with her. I never actually got to talk to him about what went on between them.

They had a confrontation and he had told her to file for divorce. He told her there was another woman in his life, and that he did not want to honor their celibacy agreement any longer. He had finally done what I had waited so long for him to do.

That same afternoon, he went out sailing and never came back—to either of us. The next day, we were supposed to get together for dinner and celebrate the first day of the rest of our lives. Instead, I got a telephone call telling me that he was dead.

After Charles died, Elizabeth came to see me and told me she knew everything, but I didn't admit anything. I know that Charles never told her it was me. If he had still been alive, I would have told her that I loved him, and I would have fought for that man. I wanted to tell her the truth, but it became a tug-of-war between us, even in death.

The hardest part was that I could not grieve for him openly. We never got to share our love among our friends.

Can you talk about your feelings about his death?
At first I thought it was some kind of plan of his to pretend he was dead to get out of his marriage. I kept expecting him to show up. When I realized what had happened was real, I was devastated. It wasn't fair. I never got to say good-bye, to kiss him one last time. It was hard to hold all that passion in for so long, waiting for the time when it could come into the light—and then to have to keep it secret even in death. I wanted to be able to express the love and joy I shared with him. Somehow I felt that verifying our love would make it real. Without bringing it into the light of day, it seemed so unreal. I didn't want to be the whore. I wanted to be loved decently. I wanted to be honored. I felt cheated that we were never able to tell the world that we loved each other.

I was angry with him that he had let that accident happen. I was angry that the only way out of the situation for him was to die. He created the whole thing. I was part of his quest. Death was just the final chapter in his ultimate adventure.

I was really angry because he was supposed to be part of my healing, but his death ripped me open. That was the hardest thing to admit, that his love was a just a band-aid over a very deep hole in my soul. I had just begun to heal the wound inside.

How has this experience changed you?

Before, I was very judgmental. Now I'm not. I was able to forgive myself for the affair I had all those years ago when I was with Frank. Forgiving myself was a very big step.

Now that Charles is not here, I close my eyes and remember our conversations. I realize now that I do deserve to be loved. I am an angel, and he loved me. And I loved him. Being morally right or wrong doesn't matter. What matters is the love. It is a gift to realize how powerful love is.

How have you been able to deal with your loss?

I have been able to tell my mother and my sister. They have been able to support me without judging me. I also found a group of people I could open up to in a safe environment. I was able to stand up and tell fifty people what happened, and allow that hole inside me to fill with love. Now I can look at a picture of Charles and not be overwhelmed with sadness. He gave me the gift of love, and it took his dying for me to surrender to it.

On our last date, I told him that he was the best lover I had ever known. Jokingly he said, "Now I can die a happy man."

Do you feel his presence in your life now?

Yes. The anger has passed, and I am looking for a way to communicate with him on a spiritual level. It feels so unfinished between us.

If you had it to do over again, what would you do differently?

I would not have held back. I would not have resisted him so much. I wouldn't have spent so much time pushing him away. Even after he left Elizabeth, I was punishing him for taking so long to make up his mind. Rather than listening to my heart, I got caught up in a power struggle. I'll never play those kinds of games again.

What is the lesson in all this?

Enjoy life and let love in. Don't play games. There is no right and wrong in love. The healing power of love can transform your life. He went for what he wanted and died a happy man.

Will you ever be able to love anyone else in the same way?

Yes. I will never try to re-create what I had with him. He opened a door for me to a dimension where love is the only thing that's real. Now I can love myself. That was his gift to me. It made me feel powerful that I could make a difference in his life.

It doesn't even matter that I didn't get to spend the rest of my life with him. It's like eating half of a dessert. At least I got to eat half of it. I got to experience a part of him that was unique. No one else shared that part of his life with him—the pinnacle of his success, his dreams and visions. I was able to know him at the source of his creative power. I will always feel the blessing of his love in my life.

It's No Fairy Tale

Over time, Joni and Ryan recognized their shared vision and surrendered to what they believed was their destined union, but Ryan was still married. Before they could be together, Joni knew that there were sacrifices to be made. In a process that took years, Joni and Ryan made a commitment to free themselves from all other entanglements. Even though they saw each other rarely during that time, their bond was forged in spirit and was an enduring one. What follows is the story of how the modern fairy tale of their romance unfolded.

Joni

Would you describe yourself as monogamous?

I have never been monogamous, but it would be my preferred mode, without question. I have a serious fear of commitment which has prevented me from being monogamous in the past. I don't think that my infidelities have been the result of some great sexual passion as much as my fear of commitment.

What does monogamy mean to you?

Monogamy means a deep soul connection to an individual whom you respect and honor on the physical, emotional, and spiritual levels. It really means that you focus all your energy into one relationship and you don't allow it to diffuse elsewhere.

Conventionally, it means sleeping with one person only, the person who is your primary partner.

What kind of stress creates a situation in which an affair is likely to take place?

When a person is frustrated in a relationship, when communication has broken down with his or her partner, and when there is sexual tension, that is the time when a person is ripe for having an affair.

But bear in mind, I have been on the receiving end of an affair. I have been the mistress. I have never been married. But when I have been unfaithful in a committed relationship, I have been unable to work through what is happening within the boundaries of the partnership.

Do you think that having an affair is immoral?

No, I don't think that having an affair is immoral. That judgment comes from the Mosaic Law of the Judeo-Christian tradition that says having an affair is committing the sin of adultery. I don't subscribe to that particular code of law.

It probably comes from a society's attempt to impose some kind of structured order, but I'm not in favor of that. For me, the state of monogamy has to be an internal reality. It has to be a decision that is constantly made, at every corner, at every turn. Without question, monogamy cannot be externally enforced.

Your personal morality is very different from conventional morality. How do you deal with the difference?

I am very fortunate in having a terrific community of friends and business associates. It has never been an issue for me. The people I attract are people who are open to different interpretations about such things.

What do you think of people who have affairs?

It depends on the person who is in it. Even though I love Ryan and am looking forward to spending the rest of my life with him, I had to work through my anger toward him for abandoning his wife, Barbara.

Do you fear that he would do the same to you?

In this world there are no guarantees. I can only be true to myself. I know what's important for me is resolving my relationship with Ryan. I need to follow this course of action that I have chosen. There is nothing else I can do. I have feelings about certain things that have happened in the past, but now it is time to move forward into the future.

How did you get involved with Ryan?

We grew up in similar places, and we have lived in similar communities. We have a similar cultural heritage that he and Barbara do not share.

When I first met them eight years ago, we were part of a community that attended functions all over the country. I would see him at meetings of all sorts. When we first met, I thought he was a pretentious snob. I had no inkling of what was ahead for us.

After that, we found ourselves together a lot of the time. And as I got to know them better, I thought that he was a really great guy, but that his wife was a mess. I wasn't so concerned at first about how he was treating her; it was more about how she was treating him. She showed him no love or affection and put him down constantly.

Barbara drank a lot, but worse than that, she couldn't handle what she drank. Some alcoholics can be well mannered when drunk, but not Barbara. I would wind up on the stairs with her, just helping her walk so she wouldn't fall into other people and begin raging. I regret this now, but once I said, "You know, I really love your husband." She answered, "I know, Joni. Everyone knows." But at that time it was just a platonic relationship. People approved of our friendship since so many of Ryan's friends were really concerned about him. At dinner parties, they would seat us next to each other.

Ryan was sweet and smart and gentle. We would talk for hours at a time, hanging out in a corner while Barbara got smashed. During the first two years, she never seemed to mind that we were spending time together. I took him off her hands so that she was free to drink. Once she found a token I had given him on his desk; she threw it out and forbid him to talk to me ever again.

He began avoiding me and I didn't know why. I was hurt, because I genuinely liked him. But I was angry too, angry with Barbara for manipulating the situation, and angry with Ryan for going along with her. I wondered why he stayed with someone so abusive.

Then about a year into our hiatus, Barbara got too high one night and almost died. She actually turned blue. I knew I could help bring her down but no one would let me go near her because they all knew she hated me. Ryan held her for hours as she thrashed about. And then later that night, after she passed out, Ryan and I went for a long walk. He told me about his home life, our imposed separation, and Barbara's sickness. That night he kissed me. Ryan remembers it as the night our affair began. I would have slept with him that night, but he had to take Barbara home.

Soon after that, Ryan got a job offer that meant moving to Tokyo. Before he moved, he asked me to join him for a vacation in Hawaii. It sounded romantic, but I realized that I was really more in love with the idea of going to Hawaii than in making a commitment to Ryan. After he sent me the airplane ticket, I changed my mind. I thought, "I can't have an affair with this guy. This is crazy." So. I ripped it up. I didn't even feel guilty about it.

What were you thinking when you ripped up the plane ticket?

That it wasn't right for me to have an affair with him. It just wasn't a healthy thing for me to do. My decision was more a matter of self-preservation than morality.

Ryan was persistent though, which is contrary to his usual Zen-like character. In most matters, he is passive. I had a business trip to Miami the next week, and when I got off the plane, who should be there to meet me but Ryan. He said he was there on business, too. So he took me to his hotel suite and that is where we consummated our affair.

I remember that we had great sex, I drank a lot, and it was not particularly earth shattering. He was older, married, and rich—and I was in way over my head. I felt as though I was in some kind of movie. I didn't really want to see him again, and I knew I wouldn't have to since he was moving overseas.

For me, the relationship really began after that. It was an old-fashioned courtship; we wrote letters and sent cards almost every week. He wrote and told me the truth about his life, his childhood, and his life with Barbara. Through his letters and poems, he confided in me in a beautiful way. We fell in love on a sacred, soul level. Our primary relationship is of the heart and soul, and not of the earth. Getting to know him in this way was like watching a flower bloom. As the truth and intimacy unfolded, I fell in love with him— even though we didn't see each other for almost a year.

We took a vacation together for only three days the next spring. We made love one night in the tantric position, sitting upright with our legs wrapped around each other, for about two hours. And the whole time I saw purple concentric circles emanating from our bodies. The power of love between us was given a life of its own that night.

We made a promise to each other that weekend: we would be together— someday. We both had things we needed to do before that could happen. I had to learn how to make a real commitment as a partner, and Ryan needed to leave Barbara. We knew it would take time, maybe years, but the promise has stood with us. About six months later, Ryan initiated divorce proceedings.

At this point, did you feel the pull of destiny between you?
Without question.

Had you felt any guilt up until this point?
Not a shred. It was blasted out of me that night we made love in Florida. I felt as though my chakras were cleaned, the goddess of love came down, kissed me on the head, and gave me the blessing of love. It was a sanctioned event after that. Anything that sacred could not be bad, and it was strong enough to absolve any shred of guilt that might have ever existed. We surrendered to a higher power and made a divine commitment to each other before God. That is what marriage should be—a marriage of the spirit.

In retrospect, what has been the gift of having an affair?
In truth, all my life I have been afraid of commitment because I was really afraid of abandonment. Infidelity has been an issue for me because of my subsequent fear to commit. It is only through the process of having a spiritual marriage first, of being with someone out of absolute choice, that I have learned how to be faithful. That has been its gift—to be able to make a commitment.

How did you deal with his wife after this?
I didn't. I was seeing someone else at the time, according to our agreement. Drew knew I was in love with Ryan, but that we couldn't be together because he was married. Also, Ryan lived in Tokyo. In spite of this,

Drew had been willing to get involved with me, although in retrospect, it was probably a mistake on both our parts.

Shortly after he filed for divorce, Ryan wanted to come for a visit and stay at my house. Out of respect for Drew, I told him that he needed to stay at a hotel and that I would see him there. He was furious! He said that if he couldn't stay at my house, he would cancel the trip, which is exactly what he did.

I was shocked by his double standard. All this time, I had made allowances for his marriage to Barbara, but he wasn't willing to do the same for me. In retrospect, I now see that I didn't understand his need for my support while he was asking for his divorce. Maybe it was due to my youth and inexperience, I don't know. Maybe it wasn't the right time for us to be together.

Anyway, I did see him later in Los Angeles. Ryan was so angry with me, I even regretted going. We went out for a drink and he yelled at me the whole night. He said that I didn't understand or appreciate what a rare and sacred union we had, and how much he had sacrificed so that we could be together.

In retrospect, Ryan admits that he was wrong. But as a result, it catapulted him back into his marriage and counseling with Barbara. He dropped the divorce proceedings. I told him that I supported his efforts to salvage his marriage with Barbara—at least to understand the dynamics of what had happened and why. And I refused to see him during that time so that he could be truly available to the counseling process. I didn't see him for almost two years.

Did you think the affair was over or was it just a phase?
It was just a phase. I knew it wasn't over. I actually wanted Ryan to go back into therapy, while I focused on my relationship with Drew. Ryan and I tried to see each other several times, but it never worked out.

How did you understand what was going on at that time?
I gave him the time he needed, knowing that it just wasn't the time for us to be together. If Ryan and I were ever going to be together, he would have to work out the situation with Barbara. I wanted him to give it a try to see if it would work.

I used to ask him why he stayed with her if he didn't love her. I asked why he didn't let go of a bad relationship and trust that life had something better for him. He couldn't understand that line of thinking at all.

Were you committed to Drew at this time?
No, I never made a commitment to Drew. Ryan had my heart, and I was never able to give it to anyone else. There wasn't enough room for me to love anyone else while I still carried him within me.

After he had been in therapy for a year, Ryan asked me to come and meet him in New York. I had very mixed feelings about seeing him. I didn't want to be in love with a married man. I didn't want to be in love with someone who couldn't be with me.

So I decided to let go of Ryan. I tried to talk myself out of it, to pawn the whole relationship off on some unhealthy urge. I asked myself all kinds of searching questions: Was I in love with Ryan because of what he could give me? Was I having an affair just because it was dangerous? Was I simply unable to commit to Drew? Did I want a married man only because he was unavailable? I put myself through a kaleidoscope of psychodrama. I did everything I could to cut the symbolic bonds between us. You name it.

I wrote him an awful letter saying that I didn't want him in my life anymore. He sent me a postcard of Marc Chagall's painting, "The Lovers." On the back he wrote, "Okay." He disregarded everything I said. Then he called and said, "Barbara's gone for a month. I want you to come stay with me." He sent me another plane ticket, and I tore it up—this time because of my loyalty to Drew. A month later, Drew and I broke up, and I felt cheated.

By this time, it had been years since we had made our promise to each other, and my doubts were becoming stronger than my faith. After my relationship with Drew, I was ready to commit to a real, full-time partnership. When Ryan asked if he could come for my birthday, I said yes.

By this time, I knew that I could not go on being his mistress, that I needed to be in a reciprocal relationship. I had to look him in the eye and say, "If you really love me and honor me, you must allow me to experience love with someone who can give it back. Unless you change your life and make yourself available to me, I can't see you anymore." He was supposed to stay a week, but left after three days. And he never said whether or not he was going to leave his wife.

Two months later, he told me he was moving out. I wondered if this time he had the courage to see it through.

Did you ever have a confrontation with Barbara?

No. She did sense he was having an affair though, but she never knew it was with me. She thought Ryan was having an affair with an old college girlfriend.

After Ryan said he was moving out, Barbara threatened to kill herself. Even though she knew the marriage was a failure, she tried everything she could to hang on to him. She begged him for another chance, so he let her stay in the house another month, which she construed as renewed hope. I questioned if it would be any easier to get her to leave in another month, but I had no choice but to trust him.

We had arranged to meet in Paris later that month, since we both had business there. We were taking a leisurely bath with a glass of wine when the phone rang. I answered it, and there was dead silence. I knew it was Barbara. She called back several times and finally demanded that Ryan tell her who the other woman was. He told her he would talk to her when he got home.

When he returned, Barbara asked him to live at a hotel for the rest of the month until she could move all of her things. She emptied all the bank accounts, took all their possessions, and moved back to the United States. It was a rough period for Ryan, but his resolve didn't melt. His bitterness toward Barbara soured everything though. He wanted me to come to Tokyo, but his rage and grief was so intense, I told him he needed to do some therapy first. I wanted to know why this had all happened. I didn't want history to repeat itself. His real work had just begun. And he agreed.

He has been going to therapy three times a week and has promised to continue for a year. His willingness to do this has awakened a profound respect for him in me. The changes he has made, of his own volition and in his own time, have allowed our relationship to bloom. Through this process, we have been able to clarify issues around respect, communication, commitment, and integrity, laying the foundation for a new kind of union for both of us.

I have been in therapy about all of this, too. We needed to see clearly though these muddy waters. Barbara is really gone, so now it is time for a new beginning. Fortunately, they have no children, and their divorce will be final soon. The settlement will be paid in a lump sum so that no further communication between them will be necessary. During their marriage of ten years, I knew them for perhaps eight, and was Ryan's lover for four.

So, it is finally our turn. I am moving in with him soon. Ironically, the time is right for me to leave my job, so I am ready for a change, too.

What has been the lesson for the two of you in all this? What have you lost and what have you gained?

Ryan's lesson, as he sees it, has been about integrity and honoring his own inner voice. He never should have married Barbara in the first place. He knew it but ignored his own intuition. Now he is learning to trust his intuition. My lessons have been many, but mostly I have learned to trust and surrender to the will of the divine.

Ryan is giving up the security of a dysfunctional relationship. I have lost the fear of making a commitment, and the fear that the universe will not take care of me. Whatever we have given up has been best for our own personal growth. I have experienced the power of love—his love, my love, our love. Love always wins in the end. Even if things don't work out for us, we will still both be further ahead.

Up until just recently, I still had doubts and questions about the future—until the last time we were together. That's when the third phase of our relationship really began. If the first phase was friendship, and the second phase was romance and courtship, now we are able to be fully present with one another for the very first time—without any fear. It was like nothing I have ever experienced in my life. Just being together was making those purple circles around the room. Again, the power of our love cleansed me of all doubt. This is it. This is love.

What is the difference between the second and third phases of your relationship?

Phase Two was the lesson. Phase Three is the opening. What I see in the future is a lot of surrendering, letting go of the past that we are both still carrying. The pain goes deeper than Barbara. Phase Three demands that we confront the barriers we erect that keep us from experiencing love. We just need time to be together, physically, and see what it's like living day to day.

Do you have any fears as you enter into Phase Three?

His cheating on me is the one fear I do not have. He never was in love with Barbara at this level. We are going into this relationship so consciously that I am very secure about how much he loves me.

Once I asked him why he had an affair with me while he was married. He answered, "To experience affection."

At some level, I fear that things won't turn out for us, that I will fall out of love. But even that carries a blessing: the freedom of having discovered a new way of being in relationship.

Do you think that being in a primary relationship together will change things ?

The affection will have to translate from a deep longing to the day-to-day reality of coexistence. The changes will be tremendous, especially since I am moving to a foreign country. I am giving away everything I own, including my job. I am going with nothing, yet I am going with everything. I am going with my love. I am being truly vulnerable, and I know the experience will be extremely transformative. All I can do is go into it as open and unencumbered as possible. Even if it doesn't work out with Ryan, I will come back a new person.

I don't know that we will be together forever. All I know is that we have work that we need to do together. There's loving that has to go down between both of us. I know that I cannot be in another partnership until I complete this one. I feel that I am experiencing true love for the very first time.

Will the prince and princess live happily ever after?
Time will tell.

Acknowledgments

To fully acknowledge all those who have inspired me to write this book means going back to my beginnings—to my parents and the life I was born to. If you believe in destiny, then writing this book is no accident. Rather it is my effort to reconcile one of the most dynamic and devastating phenomena of the human condition: love. To write about love necessitates a lifetime of experience, and even then it is a challenge to discern what is truth and what is illusion. Individually acknowledging each and every person who has influenced me on this path is an awesome task. I apologize to those I cannot name. It does not mean that your effect on my life has been any less powerful. You have not been forgotten.

To begin with, this book would never have been born without the encouragement and support of my publisher and editor, Elaine Gill. Joy Gardner deserves equal recognition for her professional and spiritual embrace, from breathing life into the initial vision to editing the final manuscript. I often compare writing a book to having a child. If this is the case, these two women have been midwives to my labors.

Thanks would be incomplete without mentioning an eclectic group of remarkable people who have provided their invaluable professional feedback: Barry and Joyce Vissell, John Gray, Stan Dale, Gordon Gordon, Carmella Weintraub, Pamela Eakins, Maia Madden, Nona Olivia, T. Mike Walker, Gregory MacNicol, and Christopher Tims. They are all teachers, healers, and writers in their own right. Each one's unique counsel and wisdom has helped me understand and respect the awesome power of love.

Needless to say, the unconditional love of friends and family is an essential element to any successful undertaking. I wish to thank all of you who have supported me throughout this process even when you didn't know what I was writing about. Nancy Gaffney, Gwen Beauregard and the Awesome Babes, Yvette Rodgers, Diane Marvin and George Koenig, Laurie Wafer and Eric Easter, Marguerite and Mark-Paul Goodman, Beth Jonquil, Virginia Arey, Eugene and Jane Wulsin, Bill and Xana Wulsin, Eugene and Tess Wulsin, Linda Wulsin, Steve and Ola Lundberg, Carol Sue Moeller, Pamela Whiting, Kali Ray, and my sailing buddies at the Santa Cruz Yacht Club are only a few of the special people whose names deserve to be seen in print. And then there are those of you whom I wish to thank whose names cannot be seen in print, especially those of who were willing to open your hearts and souls to the interview process. Your lives have given this book the rich texture of human experience that elevates it out of the realm of theory. Without you, it could not be what it is.

Last and not least I wish to acknowledge my husband Don Jacobs, whose patience, love and viewpoint has been an infinite source of inspiration even when he didn't realize it. Thank you, Don, for seeing me through all of this. You have my eternal love and gratitude.